On Becoming an
INDIVIDUAL,
A SOLDIER,
A PROFESSIONAL
LICENSED CLINICAL
SOCIAL WORKER

TRANSITIONS—A LIFELONG GRIND

VIRGINIA A. HINES, PHD, LCSW

ISBN 978-1-64140-907-0 (paperback)
ISBN 978-1-64140-908-7 (digital)

Copyright © 2018 by Virginia A. Hines, PhD, LCSW

All rights reserved. No part of this publication may be reproduced, distributed, or transmitted in any form or by any means, including photocopying, recording, or other electronic or mechanical methods without the prior written permission of the publisher. For permission requests, solicit the publisher via the address below.

Christian Faith Publishing, Inc.
832 Park Avenue
Meadville, PA 16335
www.christianfaithpublishing.com

Printed in the United States of America

CONTENTS

Foreword 5
Chapter 1. Please Allow Me to Be Me! 9
Chapter 2. How It All Began: My Military Career 14
Chapter 3. My Military Experience: Up Close and Personal 18
Chapter 4. Order My Steps: My Steps are
 Intricately Connected 36
Chapter 5. The Aleda E. Lutz Veterans Administration
 Medical Center: Social Work Roles 39
Chapter 6. Change is Synonymous with Growth 49
Chapter 7. Dissertation: Virginia A. Hines, PhD, LCSW 70
Chapter 8. Health Care for Re-entry Veterans 77
Chapter 9. Social Work Service Chief 81
Chapter 10. Veterans Administration (VA) Liaison for
 Healthcare 84
Chapter 11. Systems: Veterans Health Administration
 (Program Highlights) 87
References 95
Links 97

FOREWORD

Why A Helper?

At the age of twelve, my mother inquired, "What are you going to become when you grow up?" At the time, the answer was not as significant as the feeling of being emotionally thrust or catapult into a time in my future I had not reached. More specifically, I was encouraged even then to consider my future and my personal responsibility to myself by selecting the path I would take. Mother was always planting seeds. Planting seeds is indicative of motivating, facilitating, or elevating thought and therefore, cultivating change, growth, and development. Direction is imperative.

Fortunately, some of my classmates sought my advice when in need of consultation or feedback relative to pressing issues of our times. During my teen years, the essence of helping began to formulate the social work professional I would become. Early experiences often serve as catalyst to the formulation of ideal career paths.

Are you uncertain of your path? In view of economic uncertainty, to include the previous loss of more than eight million U.S. jobs, your answer might be yes. Why not come along with me on a remarkable journey of my life and career development as an individual, a soldier, and a Veterans Health Administration Licensed Clinical Social Worker? The journey is not for the faint at heart. The decision to become who we are meant to be is a direction for those who are goal-oriented and driven. Are you goal-oriented and driven? If you are, please do not forget to take the light with you. Light and God are synonymous. Let's go!

In memory of a virtuous woman-*Carrie*

> *Make a plan for your life. Make a plan for your life. Make a plan for your life. Be flexible. Be flexible. Be flexible. Do not be deterred. Do not be deterred. Do not be deterred. Faith that is the size of a mustard seed moves mountains. Faith that is the size of a mustard seed moves mountains. Faith that is the size of a mustard seed moves mountains!*

CHAPTER 1

PLEASE ALLOW ME TO BE ME!

Raise your left hand at the level of your face, palm should be facing away from you (outwards) with your fingers side by side. Now, look consciously at the mitten shape of your hand, which is exemplary of the view of Michigan on any U.S. map. Consider the fleshy groove linking the lower thumb and forefinger, the fleshy groove is representative of Saginaw, Michigan—down in a valley. Saginaw is ninety-eight miles north of Detroit, which is also known as the Motor City and is notorious for its linkage to the auto maker General Motors (GM) and its numerous GM plants. I recall the wonderful distinction of the four seasons and the bursts of color segway as fall leaves signal winter's soon predictably cold winter nights.

In 1979, I graduated from the Buena Vista High School in Saginaw, Michigan. I was in the top ten percent of my graduating class and knew that I would attend college. Despite feeling uncertain about the way in which my education would be financed or how I would determine the selection of the university I would attend, I was about to establish a trajectory of challenges and successes that would solidify the means by which I would complete my education and simultaneously establish my career path. Education is the key to self-determination.

Several of my classmates planned to attend college and I was no different. I scored well on my SATs and applied to Michigan State University in Ann Arbor, Michigan. I was accepted! My parents supplied funds to secure my room and board prior to the start of the school year. However, I later learned that my parents were unable to pay my college tuition. In short, I would be required to work my way through college if I wanted to attend Michigan State. My parents agreed to provide financial support. However, I was required to assume responsibility for financing my education. Question: How will you finance your education? Answer: You must find a way!

I later learned that I had been misinformed about the way in which my classmates financed their college education. In fact, most parents were not actually paying their children's college tuition. In many instances, my classmates were responsible for paying their own college tuition. Currently, there are a myriad of ways to obtain funding for college tuition. For instance, maintaining exceptional grades is often the link to scholarships and grants. While participating in community service, obtaining student loans, and entering military service are also viable options available to finance a college education. The latter would become the conduit to my graduate school education and financial independence.

During my senior year of high school, an Army recruiter visited Buena Vista High School to recruit students for military service. I do not recall how the recruiter and I began to dialog. But, interestingly, I and three of my female classmates became recruits for the United States Army. I scored well on the Armed Services Vocational Aptitude Battery (ASVAB) but really wanted to enter the Air Force. I was advised by my recruiter of a three-month wait list to enter the U.S. Air Force, so I agreed to enter the Army as a Military Police Officer in lieu of delaying enlistment. I discovered that the winning characteristics of the military included payment for college tuition, travel, monthly income, independence, and eventual linkage to employment with the U.S. Department of Veterans Affairs. I told the recruiter to sign me up! I inquired how soon I might be able to enter the Army.

Despite being recruited along with three of my high school classmates for military service, only one of us actually entered the military at the time—me. Cathy S. struggled with allergies, Cheryl B. was obese and unable to meet weight requirements, and Luerene W. did not complete high school. Hence, sealing their fates and leaving me alone to embark upon a new and exciting milestone in my life. A willingness to accept challenges in the wake of uncertainty can lead to success. Finding our own path is essential to our future. Do not be denied. Be relentless about your future…after all, it is your life!

I encountered multiple challenges to my decision to enter the U.S. Army. The challenges were linked to racial discrimination, gender bias, fear of the unknown, and misconceptions relative to the Army. Historically, the military is male-dominated and mostly undertaken by white males.

Some of my classmates doubted my sanity. Family members inquired if I were certain I knew what I was getting myself into. Fear reared its ugly head momentarily in my mother's mind. Because of my mother Carrie's faith in God, fear did not linger. Remember, my mother planted early in my mind the seed regarding the importance of my future goals for my career path. God and mother instilled in me all I needed to succeed.

Reluctantly, my mother refused to be a barrier to my certain fate. Many years later, I would learn the impact of my decision to enter the Army and delay college on my mother's life. Little did I know, I was to become a part of history; a woman of color entering an All-Volunteer Force Army during the 1970s. Many young African-American women had the same inclination that I did…join the military, serve your country, take advantage of the opportunities afforded you, obtain funds for college, and contribute to society by being the best you could be! The U.S. military is no longer male-dominant and is embraced by many women and men of color.

VIRGINIA A. HINES, PHD, LCSW

Preparing to Launch

After completing the ASVAB, all military recruits are required to pass a physical examination. Prior to departing for Detroit, Michigan, for the Army physical exam, Mother gave me a pep talk. She warned that I would encounter individuals who would want to deny me my journey. Mother instructed me to be cooperative and remember my goal. I listened, and my journey was not without incident. While waiting in line for one aspect of the physical exam, I was yelled at and ordered to move to the end of the line. I was told that I had an attitude. I followed instructions and recalled Mother's warnings. I passed the physical examination with flying colors. Keep your eyes on the prize! If we are not goal-directed, it is easy to become dissuaded and lose focus, and, hence, become unable to meet our objectives.

On September 18, 1979, I left home on a bus headed for Fort McClellan, Alabama, where I participated in Basic and Advanced Training in the U.S. Army. I was excited, yet reticent. My thoughts fell on my three classmates—wondering what their lives would become. Similarly, I pondered on my own destiny. I was not going to be deterred. There was no turning back! I was finally on my own. Transitioning from dependence to independence can be frightening, even overwhelming. Becoming independent is exciting and freeing.

Mother cautioned me to avoid bad habits (smoking, using drugs, or drinking alcohol). It was important to be cognizant of my surroundings and remain in control of myself. Being aware could serve to enhance my safety. Mother cautioned against loaning money to people. On the contrary, saving as much money as possible was imperative during military service as my future needs were undetermined. Finally, an invaluable recommendation from Mother was to avoid involvement with married men; they usually do not leave their wives. These nuggets of wisdom provided by Mother would prove invaluable investments yielding bountiful dividends to me in the coming years.

ON BECOMING AN INDIVIDUAL, A SOLDIER, A PROFESSIONAL LICENSED CLINICAL SOCIAL WORKER

Significant occurrences in my life:

- *My mother inquired of my plans for the future and supported my dreams.*
- *I completed my high school education.*
- *I prepared for college admission.*
- *I explored my options.*
- *I did not allow my classmates' negative outcomes to hinder my decision to enter the U.S. Army.*
- *Making unpopular decisions may be the key to unlock the door to your success.*

Buena Vista High School, Saginaw, MI.
Class of 1979. Keep Reaching for the Sky!

> *I am my brother and sister's keeper. I am my brother and sister's keeper. I am my brother and sister's keeper. If my brother or sister fail, I fail. If my brother or sister fail, I fail. If my brother or sister fail, I fail. If my brother or sister succeed, I succeed. If my brother or sister succeed, I succeed. If my brother or sister succeed, I succeed.*

CHAPTER 2

HOW IT ALL BEGAN: MY MILITARY CAREER

As soon as we arrived at Fort McClellan, Alabama, my fellow recruits and I were ordered to get off the bus and line up near an irate drill instructor. Our days began between 4 and 5 AM. For eight weeks, we were up and dressed in shorts or fatigues and white T-shirts, prepared for grueling physical exercise consisting of push-ups, lunges, sit-ups, and a run. Despite playing basketball and running track in high school, I was ill-prepared for the military physical training exercise program. My inability to run a quarter of a mile without falling out of formation resulted in remedial physical training. The added physical training eventually attributed to my ability to complete future runs. Becoming physically fit can be a painful, yet rewarding process.

When I entered the Army, I was 5' 9" and weighed 99 pounds. I was assigned three drill instructors (two men and one woman). The drill instructors constantly encouraged me to return for second helpings of chow. The meals were always great. I recall, affectionately, the meat and potatoes. My weight eventually increased to 120 pounds.

During basic training, I met men and women of all ages, from all walks of life and diverse cultures. My fellow women recruits were notable. Delgado was a beautiful Afro-American woman from the Dominican Republic. Kinchen was from the South. Terwalshisinkawski (uncertain if this is the correct spelling of her name), became our squad leader, and was affectionately referred to as Alphabet. Our platoon was one of the first female platoons to integrate Basic and Advanced Training with male soldiers. We were referred to as the Echo Company. The eldest drill instructor enforced the need for female recruits to stick together and avoid fraternizing with male recruits. Safety was emphasized at all times.

Female and male soldiers jointly completed physical training, learning modules, road marches, spit-shined boots, and cleaned our M16A1 rifles. Other significant tasks we learned during basic training included disassembling M16A1 rifles into component parts and re-assembling the rifle within a predetermined timeframe. Failure to complete modules in a timely manner meant the difference between graduating from Basic and Advanced Training on time and being recycled or discharged from the U.S. Army due to attrition.

Other vital modules that all recruits were required to complete included: learning the Three General Orders, responding to chemical and biological attacks, and performing first aid. During basic training, we learned the principle of "one for all and all for one". If one individual made an error, the entire unit invariably suffered repercussions for the error.

For example, there was a female recruit that was experiencing difficulty marching in formation. "Your left right! Your left right! Right face! Left face! About face!" The female recruit often turned in the opposite direction of the command rendered by the drill instructor. The entire Echo Company was advised to assist her in improving her marching skills or everyone would be marching outside during inclement weather and participating in grass drills until the female soldier could march and follow commands. The "all for one, one for all premise" permeated all aspects of our lives as soldiers. The unit quickly learned that responsibility for oneself extended beyond self and included the responsibility for our entire unit.

In basic training, female recruits were always encouraged to travel in pairs. I recall hanging out with a group of women from my unit. During a weekend pass, I and seven to eight female recruits went dancing. We rented a hotel room and stayed together. Perhaps one or two of the women went off with their significant others. I have no awareness of any of my unit female soldiers experiencing harassment or military sexual trauma (MST). Regrettably, to date, MST is a pervasive, negative aspect of military life impacting male and female soldiers (USDVA, 2015).

Women entering the U.S. military are encouraged to be careful with respect to alcohol and other drug consumption. It is no secret that substance use impairs judgment and lowers inhibition. Safety should be considered by each soldier, regardless of gender, in their units, during deployments, in their homes, and while on dates. In an environment where men outnumber women and both sexes may become victims of sexual assault, everyone is encouraged to be vigilant and aware of their surroundings and vulnerabilities.

In the event of unwanted physical (sexual harassment/assault) or verbal advances, all recruits were required to be aware of their chain of command and utilize it when warranted. If the chain of command was unwilling to address issues relevant to sexual harassment, other viable systemic supports include the Chaplain Service and the U.S. Senator or Congressional Representative in the recruit's home state of residence. Each military recruit is encouraged to maintain contact with families of origin or significant social supports in the event of challenges. Social support is vital throughout a soldier's military service and is often essential to a successful transition from military to civilian life for both male and female soldiers once enlistment is completed.

ON BECOMING AN INDIVIDUAL, A SOLDIER, A PROFESSIONAL LICENSED CLINICAL SOCIAL WORKER

Significant Lessons Learned

- *Where God provides vision he always makes provisions!*
- *There is no quit in me!*
- *We must complete each task that we undertake.*
- *MST is a pervasive issue facing military service women and men.*
- *On multiple levels women veteran continue to excel in military service.*

> *Unknowingly, we prepare for future challenges as we transcend today's obstacles. Unknowingly, we prepare for future challenges as we transcend today's obstacles. Unknowingly, we prepare for future challenges as we transcend today's obstacles. Achievement is stepping outside our safety net in the absence of knowing the outcome of our risk. Achievement is stepping outside our safety net in the absence of knowing the outcome of our risk. Achievement is stepping outside our safety net in the absence of knowing the outcome of our risk.*

CHAPTER 3

MY MILITARY EXPERIENCE: UP CLOSE AND PERSONAL

I served in the U.S. Army from September 17, 1979 through October 22, 1985. My Military Occupational Specialty was 95B10-Military Police Officer. I completed Basic and Advanced training at Fort McClellan, Alabama. The physical training and road marches were memorable as I was emotionally and physically stretched beyond normal limits. I experienced excruciating pain in my legs and hips during physical training. At times, I questioned my decision to embark upon this journey, but then I knew why I accepted the challenge—I had to do things my way. Doing things our own way usually boosts tolerance and endurance despite challenges.

During Basic and Advanced Training soldiers learned how to wear the Army uniform. Women were required to wear their hair above the bottom of their shirt collar. Combat boots and uniforms were required to be spit-shined and creased, respectively. Our daily schedule was so regimented that we scarcely had time for maintaining our boots or uniforms. For ease and comfort, I kept my hair braided under my cap and always maintained my uniform at a high standard. Due to visual impairment, I wore black cat-eyed glasses…a sight for sore eyes.

Marching and singing cadence came naturally to me. One of my favorite cadence was "Standing tall and looking good, ought to be in Hollywood! Your left, right! Up in the morning fore day, I don't like it no way!"

By the time, I completed Basic and Advance training, I could run five miles and sing/call cadence while doing so. Over the sixteen weeks of training inclusive of remedial physical training and grass drills, I learned how to breathe and concentrate, which precluded additional instances of falling out of formation (a run) and being required to participate in remedial physical training. In order to sing cadence and run in formation, learning to breathe and concentrate were essential. I was unaware that simple tasks, such as breathing and concentrating, would be crucial to my success later as I embarked upon other great challenges in my life. Often, we are preparing for future challenges as we transcend current obstacles.

I entered the military with no knowledge of firearms. As a soldier first and a Military Police Officer second, I was bound to carry a weapon. Initially, I was afraid to fire a weapon, recognizing inherent dangers and hazards associated with firearms. With proper training and supervision, I became an expert with my .38 Smith & Wesson and a sharp shooter with my M16A1 rifle. Other weapons I was required to familiarize with included: The Law, shotgun, .45 caliber handgun, grenade launcher, and nine-millimeter handgun. My favorite weapon to date remains the .38 Smith & Wesson. My military training included learning to assemble, disassemble, clean, and fire various firearms.

My advanced military training with respect to Military Police duties included: report writing, conducting search and seizure, evidence and crime scene investigation, traffic control, school guard crossing duty, and other law enforcement activities. Some of my more memorable assignments included providing security for a Brigadier General (one star) and participating in military funeral details, (which entailed executing a twenty-one-gun salute, folding the American flag, and presenting the flag to a fallen soldier's family member(s). I also enjoyed working as a Customs Inspector while serving in Europe. Custom Inspectors traveled to residences of service members departing base to inspect their household goods to ensure proper packaging and documentation of the shipment prior to its departure. The role of a military police officer continues to be vast and varied.

Responding to my very first domestic violence incident will be forever etched in my memory. While stationed at Ft. Hood, Texas (my first permanent duty station after Basic and Advanced Training) serving in the 411 Military Police Unit, Sergeant Willis and I were dispatched to base housing where a domestic disturbance was in progress. We arrived at the residence and entered a scene where we discovered a young woman standing in the middle of the living room crying and railing/waving her arms and hands uncontrollably. I observed her charred abdomen. We learned the woman accidently poured scalding hot water on herself while trying to pour the scalding hot water on her husband. There were three small children in the room crying uncontrollably. The man of the house stood nearby observing. My immediate response was to move the children and their father to a separate room where they would be removed from the chaos.

I called 911 and requested an ambulance to take the woman to the hospital. While we waited for the ambulance to arrive, I consoled the woman, assuring her that everything would be alright. When responding to domestic disturbances, it was essential to separate the parties involved, notify emergency medical service, and keep all members of the household safe. Sergeant Willis noted my quick response and subsequently submitted my name to Staff Sergeant Smith, my Platoon Sergeant, for a promotion to Private First Class (E-3). Because of my quick response and good decision-making during a dangerous situation, the crisis was de-escalated, emergency services were provided to the injured, and led to my early promotion to the next rank.

ON BECOMING AN INDIVIDUAL, A SOLDIER, A PROFESSIONAL LICENSED CLINICAL SOCIAL WORKER

I was stationed at Ft. Hood for twelve months. I had three roommates whom I became quite fond. Our ages were nineteen and twenty. My roommates and I were the only women in the unit. We resided in coed barracks and never experienced any major problems with our male counterparts. Linda P. and I were the youngest and often went out dancing together. During holidays, we participated in unit parties. My roommates and I normally palled around together. I did not smoke, drink, or use other substances. Going dancing was literally our way of having fun. Each of us ensured the other returned home safely.

One of my most memorable events was learning to drive a standard jeep. It was a challenge as Ft. Hood, Texas, has very steep hills. As a novice standard-shift driver, one of my greatest challenges was stopping on a hill and being prepared to take off in the absence of allowing the vehicle to cut off or roll backward into another vehicle. Sergeant Willis was a yeller. On one occasion while driving on patrol with Sergeant Willis, he yelled, "Private, you'd better not let this jeep roll backward!" I never did. I actually became a very good standard shift driver, and, to date, prefer to drive standard vehicles. Standard-shift vehicles often cost less and are more economic relative to gas usage.

While stationed on Ft. Hood, Texas, I honed my knowledge of law enforcement duties, which included: writing traffic citations, conducting crime scene investigations, performing guard duty, executing school guard crossing duty, performing funeral details, investigating larcenies, responding to domestic violence cases, and report writing. I carried a 38-caliber handgun, which I was never required to use during six years of active duty.

Although I often patrolled alone, I usually requested backup assistance when responding to cases. In many instances, when responding to cases with my back-up, I did the talking and the back-up officer—who was usually the patrol supervisor—was the force behind me. The patrol supervisor was usually very tall, muscular, and experienced in law enforcement activities.

A benefit of conducting law enforcement activities on military installations was military personnel usually did not wish to jeopardize their military careers, resulting in the service member's compliance when working with law enforcement to resolve an issue. The role of a law enforcement personnel is diverse and dangerous. A law enforcement personnel work very closely with fellow law enforcement officers in task completion.

Developing Close Ties

John B. and I became very good friends. His military specialty was Personnel. There were other guys in the unit. But I remember John because we occasionally went dancing with other members of our unit. When I transitioned to another station, sadly, John and I lost contact. One of the challenges of military life was maintaining contact with close friends and relatives despite the need to move occasionally. This is no longer a challenge with the advent of the Internet.

I dated two guys while at Ft. Hood. Neither of the relationships progressed beyond friendship. I imagined getting married someday. But until that time, I was not really interested in becoming seriously involved with anyone. Besides, I wanted to travel, attend college, and see the world.

Another close friend was Betty J. She was also a member of the unit. Betty J. was in a serious relationship with Tony B., a younger man. Many of the women in the unit did not understand the connection between Betty and Tony. Tony and Betty resided off base. At some point, Tony and Betty went their separate ways. After Tony had a permanent change in station (PCS), Betty and I spent more time hanging out. When I left Ft. Hood, I regrettably lost contact with Betty. The individuals I met at Ft. Hood became family to me. I was low key and enjoyed dancing, roller skating, and attending church.

Military police officers had to maintain a high standard of behavior as we wore badges and carried weapons. In addition, we worked long hours. Military police officers were required to work holidays and weekends. I wondered which direction my life would take, and if I had indeed made a good decision to enter the U.S. Army. It is normal to question our decisions during challenging times, but we must stay on course in order to succeed.

Paydays were bi-weekly or once monthly at our discretion. I opened a bank account and decided to establish an allotment that would be sent to a bank back home. Mother and I were close despite our perceived challenging relationship during my teen years. I trusted her implicitly. Mother had taken good care of the family and demonstrated great skill in managing the family finances. Mother and I made a pact. My money would be directly deposited into our joint bank account and she would maintain the bank book. I did not have any major expenses as I lived in the barracks and did not own an automobile. Many soldiers purchased vehicles and voluntarily provided rides to soldiers who did not own their own transportation. I decided to save my money. I recalled saving approximately $500 per month throughout my enlistment. I was encouraged to save as I never knew what I might need once I decided to end my time in service. Managing finances is a valuable skill that can be mastered during military service, as room and board are free for soldiers residing in the barracks.

Young people may scoff at the opportunity to travel abroad. I considered my initial PCS an opportunity to see and experience other cultures and to include exposure and access to diverse traditions, fashion, and shopping opportunities. After a year of living on Ft. Hood, my fellow roommates began to transition. Linda P. became pregnant and left the military. Another roommate was promoted and later married a fellow soldier. I transferred to Munchweiller, Germany. Munchweiller was a small post linked to a physical security site. There were few female military police officers on the base. I became accustomed to the scarcity of female military police and remained vigilant in my surroundings.

Despite the limited numbers of female military police, female soldiers were plentiful in other units. Medics, cooks, and personnel specialists were traditional military occupational specialties (MOS) for women. I made a few friends in the unit, as there were female Military Police Canine handlers in the unit who were very nice. Currently, women soldiers are assuming military occupational specialties once restricted to male soldiers (Lerman, 2013). Female soldiers continue to seek equality across military settings. The admission of women into combat roles remain a point of contention among some male soldiers.

As a military police officer in Munchweiller, Germany, fellow military policemen and I were required to catch a bus to a physical security site where we worked as physical security officers, manning observation towers. The physical security site was surrounded by a barbed wire. There were approximately eight to twelve towers strategically located around the perimeter. Inside the barbed wire fence were bunkers about eight feet tall and sixty feet in length discriminately placed around the perimeter. As a military police officer, I was required to sit in a tower for eight to twelve hours a day with my M16A1 rifle and guard chemicals.

Enclosed on the site were bunkers that contained canisters of chemicals that could be used in the event of war or other crisis. The job was not challenging until an alarm sounded, which indicated that a drill was being called and teams of military police officers were required to respond. Responding to drills required military police officers to run to designated bunkers to ensure that the bunkers were uncompromised. Physical fitness was critical to our ability to complete our assigned duties. When not manning towers, we napped, trained, or played cards.

Germany was great. When soldiers were off duty, we traveled to other destinations, ate the cuisine, and shopped on the European economy. I really enjoyed eating Yeager Snitzel, Pom Frites, and Bratwurst. My favorite drink was apple juice. Many of my fellow military police officers enjoyed the German beer. It was publicized that German beer was substantially stronger than American beer. I tasted German beer, but was never able to acquire a taste for beer. I stayed away from alcohol. Moderate ingestion of alcoholic beverages is acceptable. However, it is a huge responsibility to drink responsibly.

Shopping at a military base exchange is an awesome experience when you are young and have your own finances. In order to make any major purchases in Europe, I and my comrades had to travel to Kaiserslautern, Germany, where it turned out that there was a huge base exchange and a roller skating rink. One of my first major purchases was a Kenwood stereo set with eight components, two Bose speakers, and a glass case to contain it. In addition, I was able to purchase my first fur rabbit jacket and a small television set for my mother. At eighteen years of age, I discovered the value of earning and controlling my own finances. I planned to attend college, so foremost in my mind was the need to control my spending. However, it felt good to purchase some of the things that I wanted and give gifts to my family. I avoided frivolous spending.

All soldiers were required to take a German class and pass the driver's test in Europe. Preparing for the test was fun as many of the traffic signs consisted only of pictures with no words. An exciting aspect of European living was driving on the Autobahn. The Autobahn had no speed limit. Of course, there were accidents. But it never seemed to be an extreme number of accidents with the exception of foggy days. On foggy days, there were incidence of traffic pileups. My fascination was heightened when I discovered it was not uncommon to see Mercedes Benz, Porsche, and BMWs racing at extreme speeds on the Autobahn. Even law enforcement cars were Mercedes Benz. I imagined these roadsters began my fascination with sports cars like the RX-7, Alpha Romeo, and currently the Corvette. Despite never purchasing either of my dream cars, I did purchase a VW Beetle, a European vehicle, which I owned for twelve years.

Learning to speak German was not easy. I learned to speak a small amount of German and eventually understood more than I spoke. Speaking the language was an effort soldiers made because it demonstrated to the natives our desire to communicate with them. Most Germans could and did speak fluent English. Speaking the language was helpful when shopping or dining out. In Europe, shopping was interesting as the women dressed to the nines even to go to the market. It was an awesome experience. I loved the food, language, driving experience, shopping, and the people.

In general, Germans seemed to enjoy the presence of military installations and American citizens in their country. Military installations represented increased employment, revenue, and various other opportunities to Europeans. In turn, U.S. troops and U.S. civilians benefited as well, especially with the influx in value of the German mark (dollar). During my tour in Europe, I benefited from the mark fluctuation of up to 3.35 per American dollar. It was a great time to serve in the Army and live in Europe!

I am uncertain when or how it happened, but I met my first real love in Munchweiller, Germany. His name was Denzel C. He was a buck sergeant in a communications unit. Denzel C. was several years older than me. He was physically fit and had served in the military for several years. I remember most our shared love of dancing and music. We created dance steps to Evelyn Champaign King's, "I Been Thinkin Bout You, and There's No Doubt About it, I'm in Love." Other fun activities we shared included roller skating and shopping for my first component set. I was never so happy and was having so much fun. Denzel and I remained close for approximately eighteen months until threats to the relationship surfaced.

After working on the physical security site for more than one year, me and my female counterparts learned that women within childbearing age (eighteen to twenty-five) would be re-assigned to other positions because the chemicals we were guarding could be hazardous to our health and of our unborn children. I recall becoming alarmed…shocked. I wanted to know the details about the chemicals we had been guarding and what the ramifications to our health could be as several of us had been at the site for more than a year already. Limited explanation was provided. All of the women assigned to my unit (inclusive of me) accepted new assignments.

During one tour of duty on the physical security site, I recall observing munitions staff dressed in personal protective clothing that resembled space clothing. I observed that the canisters the staff were handling looked like bombs. Military police officers were never required to handle the canisters. Our job was to protect them. However, I was never fully educated about the type of chemical we were required to guard or the risk of exposure to me or an unborn child. I felt betrayed. My decision to sign the statement relinquishing my current duty assignment was a no brainer. Shortly thereafter, I was transferred to another location, called Pirmasens, Germany, where I was assigned to a new military police unit. Denzel and I remained close and began to consider marriage. We vowed to remain together despite the distance separating us.

In Pirmasens, Germany, I was assigned to a garrison military police unit. It was great. At some point, I was required to move to Worms (Ws were enunciated with Vs), Germany. Worms was located near the Rhine River in Europe and would be further away from Munchweiller and Denzel. He agreed to visit me. Shortly, after I moved to Worms, true to his word, Denzel came to Worms for a visit. We later became engaged to be married. My company commander agreed to allow me to return to Pirmasens to be near Denzel.

U. S. Army, Ft. McClellan Alabama,
Echo Company. Military Police Officer. 1980.

ON BECOMING AN INDIVIDUAL, A SOLDIER, A
PROFESSIONAL LICENSED CLINICAL SOCIAL WORKER

Those Are the Breaks!

Everything was going well between Denzel and me until we went to his hometown to meet his family en route to my home, Saginaw, Michigan, where we were to be wed. The wedding was planned and things were set. We arrived in South Carolina. Denzel's mother greeted me coolly. His sister was cordial. A disagreement ensued between Denzel and his mother. She conveyed her dissatisfaction about the wedding. I learned that Denzel had been sending an undisclosed sum of money to his mother from his monthly military income. His mother was not happy that the checks would be discontinued after our wedding. I was very hurt about the discussion I overheard and requested to be moved to a hotel. Denzel was okay with my request, but did not stay with me. I called my mother upset and crying and she suggested that I come home.

I returned the engagement ring to Denzel prior to my departure. We both cried as we decided to end the engagement and the relationship. It was my first major relationship loss. I made an impulsive decision to give up someone that I loved instead of fighting for him. It was a huge mistake on my part. I went home to my family. My mother gave me a pep talk and verbalized her surprise that I was not "all broken up" over the breakup. I was home with family, and that helped me cope with my loss.

In a week I returned to Europe. Upon my return, I spoke with my commander informing him of the thwarted engagement. The commander agreed to allow me to return to Worms. I saw Denzel twice more prior to my return to Worms. He and I were both hurt. Perhaps he wanted to hurt me more as he let me know that he never really loved me in the first place. I was devastated. Our last encounter was at the post office where he inquired where I was moving. I advised him "it really did not matter." I left and never looked back. But to this day, I never think I met another man that I bonded with as well or loved more. He used to say, "be strong you are with me." I recall being down about the slow process of being promoted to sergeant. Denzel took me down town Worms to buy me flowers in efforts to cheer me up. I thought that was a real gesture of love and concern.

I had been in Germany for three years and six months. During my stay in Worms, I guarded a Brigadier General (one star). Everywhere he went, I went, carrying my .38 Smith & Wesson. Fortunately, I never had to draw my weapon. Other duties were garrison (routine law enforcement) military police duties. I had a great time. Just as I was ready to leave Europe, I was involuntarily extended due to a shortage of Military Police in Europe. I remained in Europe for a total of four years.

My next duty station was Ft. Dix, New Jersey. It was to be my last stop before my six years of service ended. The battalion commander had an artillery military specialty. He was accustomed to spending a great deal of time in the field (woods) conducting training exercises. The battalion commander also enjoyed long physical training runs each morning, which I no longer minded as I had no problem running in formation due to my previous remedial training. However, living in the woods was not my preference for several reasons…the field meant living in tents and being cold. These were the times I questioned my decision to enter the Army. Luckily, field duty was usually the exception rather than the norm.

I became a squad leader after finally being promoted to the rank of Sergeant. There were ten to eleven men in my squad. We never knew when we would be required to go to the field. Shortly after being promoted to Sergeant, in the midst of winter, my unit was advised by the battalion commander to prepare for a week in the field. I recall that it was extremely cold. It seemed as if I was cold the entire time we were in the field.

Our unit was advised to take extra pairs of socks and encouraged to change our socks regularly, as no one would be permitted to return to the unit due to cold injuries. I constantly checked on my squad members and reminded them to change their socks often. However, I was only able to change my socks once.

Field training consisted of playing war games, patrolling, formulating goals to achieve objectives, determining rally points, and always evaluating on ways we might improve. Our unit did not get much sleep during the exercise because we were constantly on patrol. I learned the significance of having a plan (A, B, and sometimes C) as plans do not always go as desired.

My military police unit remained in the field for approximately one week. I recall getting into the shower as soon as possible upon my return from field duty. I noticed immediately that my feet began to swell and I was unable to walk. I was immediately taken to the hospital. I became alarmed when I learned from the physician that there was a possibility that I could lose some toes or perhaps both feet. I was very afraid as I had no feeling in either of my feet. I called my mother, who immediately chastised me for failing to take care of myself. The physician felt that I should remain in the hospital for a few days. I begged the physician to allow me to return to the barracks as I had my own room. The physician agreed to allow me to return to the barracks with reservations. I was given strict directives about remaining on bed rest. I was required to return to the hospital for a follow-up in a couple of days. I used crutches to assist with ambulation as both feet were numb.

I was on bed rest for several days, but I noticed that my feet remained numb. I was given a profile by the podiatrist that disallowed running and required that I wear tennis shoes for two to three months. Eventually, the feeling in my feet gradually returned. It was two to three months before I was permitted to try running in formation. When I did receive authorization, running was very painful. I preferred feeling pain rather than having my toes or feet amputated. I endured. Finally, I returned to full duty and was able to wear my combat boots and run in formation again. However, to date, I have cold restrictions for my feet that remain a part of my military medical records. I am fortunate to be able to walk today.

During my tour of duty at Ft. Dix, I met a man that I would later marry—Benny S. He was a fellow military police officer. I loved Benny. We were so young. Benny was nice, did not drink alcohol or smoke, and we began to hang out together along with other friends. After a year, I learned that I had orders to return to Europe. Benny S. also received orders notifying him that he would be returning to Europe as well. We vowed to keep in touch with one another. I was stationed in a place called Bad Kreuznach, Germany, and Benny S. was stationed in Swineford, Germany. A grave distance separated Benny and I, however, we did manage to reconnect.

Frequently, military personnel meet and marry quickly. Sometimes, couples are truly in love. In other instances, marriage can be attributed to financial gain. Soldiers usually obtain base housing and additional income when they are married and have children. I was not interested in marriage at this point. I still had plans to attend college after the military. Benny S. and I became close and eventually became engaged.

I was transferred to Bad Kreuznach, Germany where I became a Customs Officer. Our role encompassed performing inspections of household goods exiting and entering Europe. My three colleagues and I were supervised by a staff sergeant. I was responsible for assigning work and maintaining the documentation. My colleagues actually conducted the inspections.

Due to a shortage of base housing, I was permitted to live off base. I found a one-bedroom efficient apartment within walking distance of the base. Some of the factors that contributed to my great time in Europe included my ability to pay for airline tickets for my parents to travel to Europe for their 34th wedding anniversary and my parents were able to meet Benny S.—my significant other.

Benny S, my parents, and I toured Paris and were able to see memorable landmarks like the Eiffel Tower, The Louvre, and the Arc de Triomphe. Mother brought an empty suitcase to Europe and we shopped until she became tired of spending the German Mark. Mother left Europe with some unique styles that included red leather boots and a matching red leather jacket. Dad ate as much cheese, bread, and meat as he could. We had an awesome time. Benny and I enjoyed the time we spent with my parents.

In 1985, my enlistment in the Army neared an end. I completed my research of university locations, areas of study, and college costs. I discovered that Ferris State University in Big Rapids, Michigan, was close enough to my parents that I could visit family and far enough away to maintain my independence. In addition, Ferris was an accredited University with a Social Work Program.

ON BECOMING AN INDIVIDUAL, A SOLDIER, A PROFESSIONAL LICENSED CLINICAL SOCIAL WORKER

During military service, I participated in the Veterans Educational Assistance Program (VEAP), which was a matching program. For every dollar I saved, the government matched it with two dollars to support my college education. After six years in the Army, I had enough money to pay for a bachelor's degree. In addition, I amassed thousands of dollars in savings to secure my future during and post completion of college.

To facilitate my enrollment in college, I took leave from the Army and returned home to Michigan. I visited family briefly. I then took a bus to Big Rapids, Michigan, where I participated in a tour of Ferris State University. I enrolled in Ferris University and returned to Europe. I ended my tour of service (ETS) and returned to Ft. Dix, New Jersey, where I was officially discharged honorably from military service. In the winter of 1985, I was discharged from the U.S. Army. Four days later, I began classes at Ferris State University. Planning your future and making sacrifices, such as serving in the military and saving your money to facilitate decision-making, is empowering and rewarding.

Many of my Army colleagues in Europe did not believe that I was going to transition out of the Army, especially Benny S. I made everyone aware that I had a plan for my future that encompassed attending college. I departed Europe with an engagement ring on my finger from Benny S. He promised to send me his car to ensure that I had transportation to and from college. Shortly after my end term in service, Benny S. also ended his term in service and moved to Big Rapids, Michigan. Benny decided to draw unemployed and eventually he began to seek employment. The military taught me the importance of planning and follow-through. It is not essential that everyone support your plans. However, it is imperative to have a plan.

I maintained twelve to fourteen credit hours of college course work and maintained my grade point average as I strived to obtain my bachelor's degree in Social Work. Benny S. struggled to find employment in Big Rapids, Michigan. At times, Benny S. seemed to lack motivation. I was focused on my studies, and he focused on obtaining employment. Benny worked sporadically. We married in

1986. The marriage was troubled as Benny S. and I had different goals. In 1988, one of Benny S.'s friends invited him to Maryland to assist him with employment. I discovered that Ferris would permit me to complete my final course in Maryland if desired. I found a university in Maryland that would allow me to transfer in to complete my remaining course. Benny S. found employment with the Defense Intelligence Agency. But our relationship remained strained. I obtained an Associates of Pre-Arts and a Bachelors of Social Work from Ferris State University in 1989. Despite challenges, we must complete what we start.

While completing my final course of study at Bowie State University, I met a university instructor who made me aware of an opportunity to obtain a scholarship and a grant to obtain my Master's degree in Social Work through the University of Maryland. Interestingly, I never thought of getting a Master's degree until the opportunity presented itself. But, had I never obtained the Bachelor's degree, it would have been impossible for me to walk into the blessing of a Master's degree and, later, a Doctorate degree. I was ecstatic!

In order to obtain the Masters of Social Work (MSW), I would be required to attend the University of Maryland for two more years. Benny S. emphasized the urgency for me to obtain employment. I had been attending college for four years and needed full-time employment. Money to fund the MSW was not an issue. I still had money for college emanating from military service, and the MSW would be fully funded by a grant and a scholarship. Benny expressed a desire to have a child. I was not ready for a family at that point. I felt that married couples should have joint goals in addition to individual goals. It was becoming increasingly evident that Benny S. and I were going in different directions.

One day, Benny S. informed me that he could see that I really wanted to obtain my MSW. He therefore granted his approval. Prior to getting Benny S.'s final support to begin college, I was advised that I needed surgery. I had multiple fibrous tumors in my uterus that needed to be removed. Benny and I met with the doctor and she advised us that if I had become pregnant, I would have lost the baby due to the volume of fibrous tumors in my uterus. The doctor advised me that she would perform a laparotomy and try to remove as many tumors as possible. I had the procedure prior to the start of the MSW program at the University of Maryland, Baltimore Campus. Shortly thereafter, Benny and I divorced.

Significant Lessons Learned

- *Attention to details and high performance on the job can be financially and personally rewarding.*
- *The military provides training, income, and relationships that foster personal development.*
- *Military service can serve as a conduit to college and employment opportunities.*
- *Staving off self-gratification is a challenge but may lead to better career and educational options in the future.*
- *Saving money while in the military can provide financial security that is sustaining during later phases in the life cycle.*
- *Possessing desire is half of what is required to complete any task successfully.*

> *Don't stagnate. Get ready! Don't stagnate. Get ready! Don't stagnate. Get ready! When the door of opportunity opens, walk through it. When the door of opportunity opens, walk through it. When the door of opportunity opens, walk through it. Think, plan, execute. Think, plan, execute. Think, plan, execute!*

CHAPTER 4

ORDER MY STEPS: MY STEPS ARE INTRICATELY CONNECTED

I attended the University of Maryland at Baltimore from September 1, 1989 to June 4, 1991. I obtained a Master's of Social Work degree. In addition, I participated in a twelve-month internship at the Ft. Howard VA Medical Center in Baltimore, Maryland. It was during the internship that I learned my veteran status and the completion of the internship at Ft. Howard afforded me priority hiring with any VA that had vacancies for social workers for up to one year after completion of the internship. I was amazed that my steps were ordered and intricately connected through God's grace. I marveled at the way in which entering the U.S. Army and serving for six years was paying off in dividends. Favor, nothing but God's favor! Saving my money and participating in the VEAP Program allowed me to pay for my Bachelor's and Associates degrees. Had I not obtained my Bachelor's degree, I could not have been eligible to walk through the door to obtain my Master's degree (grant and scholarship). Moreover, the internship provided a conduit to employment with the Veteran's Health Administration.

I was blessed to be reared by awesome parents who permitted me and my siblings to be children during our childhood and permitted time to focus on education and enjoyment of our youth. My parents were examples of great decision-making, safety, and provision of basic needs essential to mine and my sibling's development. I was able to grow up, formulate my own decisions, and make the best choices for my own life. Invariably, mistakes occur. Mistakes made by responsible individuals are usually tolerable. I was taught early that when I make a mistake, I should correct it as soon as I realize I've made the mistake. In short, avoid remaining in a mistake long term. Risk-taking and self-confidence are individual traits intrinsic to survival and goal attainment.

There were no available positions for social workers at The Ft. Howard VA Medical Center when I graduated from the University of Maryland. However, during my second year of graduate school I completed a second internship at the Jessup Women's Correctional Institution in Jessup, Maryland. The internship lead to full-time employment. Surprisingly, the position was short-lived due to budget cuts. Me, along with thirty other social workers prayed for new employment. I secretly vowed to God, if he allowed me to find other employment I would tithe my income. My greatest fear was being required to return home without employment; becoming a burden to my parents. But God showed up and showed his majesty!

I prayed and continued to seek employment. I submitted an application to the Social Work examining unit through usajobs.gov—the premier federal website for federal employment. Anxious to find employment, I applied for a social work position with Johns Hopkins Medical Clinic in downtown Baltimore, Maryland. I was selected for a position in outpatient social work and I remained at the clinic for one year. Almost a year to the date that I submitted my application for federal employment, I received notification from the examining unit that there was a social work vacancy in Saginaw, Michigan, at the Aleda E. Lutz VA Medical Center. I was going home!

VIRGINIA A. HINES, PHD, LCSW

Significant Lessons Learned

- *Identifying goals and planning execution of objectives does not guarantee success.*
- *Being connected to all power (the only true and living God) guarantees success!*
- *I am not in control of myself or my life. I acquiesce to God!*
- *When trouble comes do not give up! Do not falter or succumb to the crisis. Stand in God.*
- *When I make one step, God makes multiple steps. Glory!*

> *Work while it is day. Work while it is day. Work while it is day. Hard work pays off. Hard work pays off. Hard work pays off. Stay focused. Stay focused. Stay focused. Systems are composed of integrated parts that work together towards a common goal. Systems are composed of integrated parts that work together towards a common goal. Systems are composed of integrated parts that work together towards a common goal.*

CHAPTER 5

THE ALEDA E. LUTZ VETERANS ADMINISTRATION MEDICAL CENTER: SOCIAL WORK ROLES

Inpatient Medicine: Discharge Planning

I was hired at the Aleda E. Lutz Veteran Administration Medical Center (VAMC) in Saginaw, Michigan, my hometown. My employment at the VA in Saginaw spanned from 1992 to 1997. How fabulous! I had three other social work colleagues Pam (deceased), William, and Peg (currently in a nursing home). The latter took me under her wing and taught me the essentials of veteran benefits, which enhanced my knowledge of medical social work. My employment assignments while at the Aleda E. Lutz VAMC included: Inpatient Medicine, Intensive Care Unit, Nursing Home Care Unit, Community Nursing Home Program, and Visual Impaired Services

Team (VIST). I gained vast social work experience while employed at the Aleda E. Lutz VAMC.

The Veterans Health Administration (VHA) is the largest employer of Masters-prepared social workers in the nation (USDVA, 2016). The VA social work role has evolved over ninety years. As a social worker assigned to an inpatient medical unit, I was responsible for conducting initial psycho-social assessments of all new patients within twenty-four hours of their admission to the hospital. The goal was to identify veterans at risk of homelessness and lacking resources or social supports that might invariably lead to re-hospitalization after discharge. Female veterans were considered at risk by virtue of the limited number of females on inpatient units at VAs and gender issues relative to treatment in VA medical centers. Gender issues were relative to the male-dominated populations traditionally served at VAs, the historic focus on male veterans and male veteran health issues, the lack of privacy for women veterans at VA, the lack of female pajamas, the limited knowledge of female health-related issues by male physicians, the low number of female physicians, the limited number of examination rooms for female veterans, and the limited amount of supplies for female veterans.

The number of women veteran treated at VA healthcare facilities has doubled as a result of the wars in Iraq and Afghanistan (USDVA, 2017). Hence, healthcare services delivered to women veterans treated at VAs are enhanced and expanded to address issues to include, but not limited to, health, benefits, housing, military sexual trauma, and traumatic brain injury. Most of the previous barriers to women veterans seeking healthcare at VA have been eradicated.

Social workers are essential when linking veterans to VA and community services prior to discharge from VA facilities. VA resources include but are not limited to: substance abuse treatment, mental health services, nursing home placement, caregiver support, MyHealtheVet, suicide prevention, veteran's choice, and tele-medicine (USDVA, 2016). VA is credited with an ability to evolve in response to the ever-increasing needs of soldiers, veterans, and family caregivers. The VA's mission is to provide quality services to veterans and their caregivers (USDVA, 2016). The wars in Iraq and

ON BECOMING AN INDIVIDUAL, A SOLDIER, A PROFESSIONAL LICENSED CLINICAL SOCIAL WORKER

Afghanistan continue to spur the VA's efforts to improve service delivery to soldiers, veterans, and their caregivers.

A major responsibility I had as a VA social worker was and continues to be discharge planning. Discharge planning usually requires weekly participation in interdisciplinary team meetings inclusive of veterans, family members and/or caregivers, and other ancillary service providers. The cusp of discharge planning is that the process begins at the time a veteran is hospitalized and continues until discharge. The veteran and their support systems are intricately involved in the discharge planning process. In addition to veterans and family supports, discharge planning usually includes but is not limited to a physician, a pharmacist, nurses, nutritionists, and physical therapists. It is essential that interdisciplinary teams customize treatment plans to mirror the level of care that each veteran requires to live in the least restrictive environment upon discharge. Hence, team communication is essential in the formulation of a treatment plan conducive to veteran self-determination and the veteran's ability to live in the least restrictive environment upon discharge from a VA medical center or other setting.

During veteran hospitalizations, I performed a social work task which consisted of assessing the veteran's interest in and mental competency to complete an advanced directive. Advanced directives are designed to assist the veteran with documenting healthcare preferences in the event of mental or physical incapacitation. Advanced directives also outline the veteran's interest in life-sustaining measures, which prolongs life despite the presence of a terminal diagnosis. Advance directives afford veterans the opportunity to designate a medical power of attorney (POA) for health care as desired. A medical POA ensures veteran-documented treatment preferences relative to life-sustaining measures are executed as the veteran requested while mentally competent. The veteran have the right to decline execution of an advanced directive.

Veterans discharged from VA hospitals often require ongoing medical services (i.e., intravenous medications, wound care, physical therapy, occupational therapy, speech therapy, personal care, or assistance with activities of daily living). Social workers assigned to medical, surgical, intensive care, and community living centers of VA medical centers are crucial when coordinating discharge planning services with the veterans and their families. Moreover, joint coordination between all disciplines involved in discharge planning is crucial to successful veteran-centric care and discharge of veteran to the least restrictive environment.

When the veteran are unable to return home due to the need for continuous (24 hour) skilled nursing care, social workers coordinate nursing home placement options with veteran and veteran caregivers to ensure quality care and close proximity to loved ones. To facilitate nursing home placement, I was required to have knowledge of contracts and provider agreements, rates for care, eligibility for services, and required documentation. Essential to implementation of a nursing home placement is the social worker's ability to assist the family with coping with the veteran's loss of independence. Social workers must have knowledge of alternative placement options (group homes, state veteran homes, domiciliary, and Department of Housing and Urban Development VA Supportive Housing [HUDVASH]) which serve as conduits to the progressive transition of veterans to the most appropriate least restrictive placement.

As a VA social worker, I not only coordinated nursing home placements; I conducted nursing home follow-up to ensure that veterans received quality healthcare. I coordinated notification of the facility physician and the assigned VA provider to convey veterans' need for specialty services or prosthetic equipment. Furthermore, I ensured that the veteran/caregivers remained supportive of the placement. Social workers lead the inspections of contract nursing homes during scheduled intervals to ensure that nursing homes maintain state certifications and continue to deliver quality services to our nation's veterans. Should nursing homes lose accreditation or fall under other scrutiny, the VA has the capability to relocate veterans to other accredited facilities, pending corrective actions.

Community Living Centers (Nursing Home Care Units)

VA medical centers often have community living centers (CLC) attached to their facilities. CLCs are designated for short-term rehabilitation, respite care, long-term hospice, or permanent stays (usually reserved for veterans with service-connected disabilities [SC]). SC disabilities include injuries acquired prior to military service that are exacerbated and injures acquired during active duty. Veterans with SC disabilities receive compensation for their conditions.

Social workers are gatekeepers for admission to CLCs, as social workers conduct clinical assessments, facilitate family council meetings, assist with coordination of admissions and discharges along with a litany of other activities. Additional social work duties include, but are not limited to, contacting adult protective services, linking veteran to veteran service organizations for assistance, completion of advanced directives, and assisting with compensation and pension issues.

CLC residents admitted for longer term stays require re-assessment at specified intervals. Social work re-assessments are usually warranted when residents experience a change in health status or other instances that may inhibit discharge to the least restrictive environment.

Family members of CLC residents experience ups and downs with respect to alterations in the health status of their veteran family member. CLC residents' health often improves when meals, medication, personal care, and other activities of daily living (bathing, grooming, and toileting) are provided at regularly scheduled intervals. Hence, it is not uncommon for veterans to enter and exit CLCs on a recurrent basis. During CLC admissions, veteran usually experience improved health status, due to regular and timely assistance with meals and activities of daily living. Similarly, the health status of a family caregiver usually fluctuates (improves or declines) when veterans enter or exit CLCs.

VIRGINIA A. HINES, PHD, LCSW

Family Council

Family members and/or caregivers experience disruptions in health maintenance, sleep, and recreation during the veteran's CLC admissions/discharges. Family council meetings are used to help mediate family member's stress. VA social workers facilitate family council meetings and usually invite each family member of CLC residents to participate in the monthly meetings.

The social worker and family members benefit if the family counsel is held monthly. Family council is the vehicle used by both the family member and the social worker to build rapport. Moreover, the council meetings provide a space where family members can become familiar with VA services, policies related to the CLC, discuss discharge planning, and alterations to discharge plans.

An essential and supportive aspect of family council is that it allows family members to interface with each other, thereby, normalizing the family member experience. Often, family members bond, develop a personal support network, and learn that they are not alone in coping with a chronically ill veteran that is constantly entering and exiting the CLC.

While assigned to the CLC at the Aleda E. Lutz VAMC, I observed alterations in the life cycles of my assigned veterans. Family members often displayed limited knowledge of illness processes, inclusive of death and dying. During the life cycle, veterans often experience multiple admissions to VA hospitals and CLCs. Spouses are constantly required to make life and activity adjustments to cope with the changing needs of the veteran. Spouses in turn require support. Spouses often exhibited anger and resistance to taking the veterans on outings, weekend passes, or home permanently when the veteran's stay in the CLC concluded. To avoid last-minute alterations to discharge plans and recognition of impaired coping or resistance prior to the date of discharge, social workers engage family members during family council to verify and re-verify the veterans discharge plans. The verification of the discharge plan should be done frequently and throughout the CLC placement.

Death and Dying Support Group/Psycho-Education

In an effort to provide support to family members of CLC residents, I developed a family support group for caregivers of CLC residents coping with death and dying. Utilizing Dr. Elizabeth Kubler-Ross's book, *On Death and Dying*, and PowerPoint slides, family members were educated about the stages of death and dying and introduced to various reactions of dying patients and their families to terminal illnesses. The role of social workers includes identification of unmet needs of the veterans and family members and developing services to circumvent unmet needs. Continuous participation in support groups afford family members space to discuss concerns and uncomfortable feelings. Social workers facilitating support groups are afforded opportunities to monitor family concerns and facilitate preparation for alterations in veteran health status, to include coping with end of life matters.

VIRGINIA A. HINES, PHD, LCSW

Visual Impaired Services Team

I was a member of a Visual Impaired Services Team (VIST) that consisted of two social workers and a VIST coordinator. We met at scheduled intervals with blinded and visually impaired veterans and their families. The goal was to facilitate admissions to blind rehabilitation schools, identify needs for prosthetic equipment, and to identify participants for the VA winter games. The social work role encompassed assisting visually impaired and blinded veteran with placement in handicap-accessible housing and linkage to other vital services to include, but not limited to Homemaker Home Health, Adult Day Health Care, and Meals on Wheels. Social workers are essential in linking veteran to internal VA services as well as external community resources.

ON BECOMING AN INDIVIDUAL, A SOLDIER, A
PROFESSIONAL LICENSED CLINICAL SOCIAL WORKER

Social Work Advocacy

Social workers often interface with patient advocates who are frequently contacted by disgruntled veterans or veteran caregivers relative to timeliness and quality of care issues. When veterans are advised of referrals for upcoming appointments that are not received in a timely manner, veterans are encouraged to seek assistance from their primary care teams. However, if services are delayed after notification of primary care providers, veteran reserve the right to seek additional assistance through the patient advocate.

Quality-of-care issues might include, but are not limited to, availability of specialty services or procedures, timely discharge from hospitals or CLC's, possible patient's rights violations, or alleged patient abuse issues. In efforts to resolve timeliness and quality-of-care issues, complaints are often filtered to social workers and attempts are made to resolve issues with veterans and veteran caregivers in the best interest of the veteran.

During my employment at the Aleda E. Lutz VAMC, I was selected as the Employee of the Month and Employee of the Year. I was able to meet the Secretary of the Department of Veteran Affairs, Jesse Brown (deceased). Hard work does not go unnoticed. When completing daily assignments, it is crucial for social workers to concur with professional ethics. It is vital that patient care is prioritized and conducted in accordance with clinical practice guidelines. It became apparent that my colleagues and other professionals noted my professionalism and the quality of care provided to my patients. I remain immensely proud of my awards and the love and respect provided me by the interdisciplinary team at the Aleda E. Lutz VAMC.

During my fifth year of employment at the Aleda E. Lutz VAMC, changes began occurring on multiple levels. The social work chief took another position. Subsequently, a new chief was hired. One of my senior colleagues became ill and demonstrated some difficulty completing her daily tasks. In short, it is crucial for social workers, and other professionals within the VA healthcare system, to work collaboratively to ensure quality service delivery to veterans, and family caregivers. When we encounter an impaired colleague, it is crucial that social workers facilitate the impaired colleague's receipt of assistance by reporting their impairment to the immediate supervisor in order to ensure client safety, as well as staff safety. Options include approaching the impaired colleague to inquire if we can provide assistance, as we notice alterations in functioning; contacting the social work supervisor who can be instrumental in referring an employee to the Employee Assistance Program; and contacting the Board of Social Work to report the impaired employee. Social work chiefs or supervisors are able to request a fitness-for-duty evaluation of employees exemplifying alterations in functioning to solidify wellness and quality social work service delivery to veteran, service members, and family caregivers.

Significant Lessons Learned

- *Serving in the U.S. military provides an avenue to fund a college education for veterans and their families.*
- *The U.S. military provides access to a myriad of benefits to include, but not limited to, housing, federal employment, retirement, and a litany of other benefits.*
- *The social work role is variable and transcends work sections within VA.*
- *Quality service delivery and attention to detail in the provision of social work services to veterans, service members, and family caregivers is rewarding.*
- *Services exist within the Veterans Health Administration to identify and link impaired social workers to services that facilitate wellness and ensure quality service delivery to veterans and their caregivers.*
- *Social workers and patient advocates often work collaboratively to resolve veteran timeliness of care and quality of care issues.*

> *Master major milestones in order to ascend to your God-given destiny. Master major milestones in order to ascend to your God-given destiny. Master major milestones in order to ascend to your God-given destiny. What's holding you back? Face it head on! What's holding you back? Face it head on! What's holding you back? Face it head on! Look UP! Look UP! Look UP!*

CHAPTER 6

Change is Synonymous with Growth

Seeking Federal Employment (Helpful Hints)

Life encompasses occasions when we must step outside the arc of familiarity and complacency to venture into unchartered territory or new directions if we really want to experience success. Close family members and friends may question our decision to challenge the status quo. However, remaining goal-oriented, God fearing, and a lifelong learner are characteristics essential to success. Where there is a yearning to learn, there is potential to move, evolve, and defy limits. I recognized a need to continue to grow and I did.

I learned of a federal employment website called usajobs.gov. The website permits users to develop up to five resumes online and complete federal applications for civil service employment. Applications and supporting documents to include diplomas, certificates, DD214 (military discharge papers), and other federal documents can be submitted to respective employers quickly, making it possible for veterans and non-veterans alike to obtain gainful employment and benefits through federal employment. Federal employment opportunities are vast, promotions are possible, but travel may be required. It helps if applicants are mobile.

Obtaining gainful employment is increasingly competitive. Technological advances made possible through the Internet improves the speed of application submission and processing. Conversely, the Internet virtually eradicates visual and communication nuisances in the absence of meeting prospective employers face to face during employment seeking. How does someone demonstrate interest in employment? How do applicants make their application more noticeable amid hundreds of applicants for the same job in the Internet era?

Individuals seeking federal employment need to be aware that it takes time to prepare a quality resume. It is expedient to submit multiple applications to multiple federal agencies. Multiple application submissions to multiple federal agencies is strongly recommended (aggressive application submission, may be exemplary of fifteen to twenty application submissions per day until interviews are scheduled, is recommended). Interviewing may be stressful, but effective listening and addressing all aspects of interview questions is highly recommended and may be instrumental in helping you obtain your dream job. Performance-based interviewing highlights: What did you do? How did you do it? Who helped you? List the ways your performance impacted your employer's bottom line. Finally, share with prospective employers any accolades you received as a result of your performance (e.g. raises, promotions or other benefits). Applicant responses to the aforementioned questions serve as an adequate guide when responding to interview questions and building an effective resume.

Interviews for federal employment may be completed face to face or via the telephone. It may take several months to actually obtain federal employment. However, obtaining federal employment and federal benefits are worth the wait.

While vacationing in Las Vegas, Nevada, I decided to visit the VA. Las Vegas is anesthetically beautiful. The temperatures exceed

ON BECOMING AN INDIVIDUAL, A SOLDIER, A PROFESSIONAL LICENSED CLINICAL SOCIAL WORKER

115 degrees Fahrenheit during the summer months. The plethora of thematic hotels and casinos titillate your senses and encourage thoughts like: What would it be like to live, work, and play in Las Vegas? When gambling, it is important to recognize that the odds always favor the house. Therefore, living and working in Las Vegas would not be problematic for me as I was not and remain a non-gambler.

When I arrived at the VA, wearing summer attire, I was self-assured that Las Vegas would one day be my home. "Mr. D-the Chief of Social Work at the time, was in a meeting but willing to meet with me as soon as he was available. I agreed to wait. When traveling, I usually carried a copy of my federal application as there was no way to determine who I might encounter in airports or during flights. When Mr. D. became available I was privy to an unplanned interview. I shared my short-term and long-term employment goals with Mr. D. (five years and later). Essentially, I conveyed my interest in serving veterans, continuing my education and remaining an advocate for families of service members. My ultimate goal was and remains to retire from the VA. Mr. D. was pleased with my responses. He accepted my application and expressed his inability to offer me a position that day, but he encouraged me to remain in contact with him.

After meeting Mr. D, I felt excited about my potential to obtain employment with the Las Vegas VA. I pledged to maintain contact with Mr. D. Two weeks later, I sent Mr. D. a thank you note as he had spent more than an hour with me during our initial meeting. I emphasized my continued interest in employment with the Las Vegas VA. I vowed to maintain contact with Mr. D and provided my address and a valid telephone number in the event of a vacancy. Two months later, I called Mr. D. and expressed my continued interest in employment. He still had no vacancies. However, six months later, I received a call from a human resources representative of the VA offering me a position at the Las Vegas VA. I began employment as an inpatient social worker at the VA Las Vegas on December 22, 1997.

Persistence pays! Obtaining a master's degree in social work after completing six years of military service caught the employer's attention immediately. My willingness to transfer from Saginaw to Las Vegas was an added strength because many employers want employees who can fill vacancies immediately. When employees take on new projects that benefit their employer's bottom line, employers note employee creativity and motivation to enhance service delivery; creating a win-win situation. The fact that I received two awards during the same calendar year suggested I was a hard worker that other employees in the organization recognized and respected.

Making a face-to-face contact or completing an interview with prospective employers are great opportunities to market yourself. However, maintaining contact with a prospective employer and working in the area or field in which you are seeking federal employment facilitate selection for federal employment. Moreover, a willingness to saturate federal agencies with applications on usajobs.gov will enhance selection probability. I must emphasize, a one-application submission may not invariably get you the job you seek. Push the limits. I have submitted between seven and twenty applications in one day on usajobs.gov during employment-seeking intervals. The larger the number of job applications submitted by an applicant, the greater the probability of the application being viewed by multiple employers. Hence, increasing the likelihood of your being interviewed and hired for federal employment.

ON BECOMING AN INDIVIDUAL, A SOLDIER, A
PROFESSIONAL LICENSED CLINICAL SOCIAL WORKER

Southern Nevada Healthcare System (1997–2011)

Inpatient Medicine and Surgery

I arrived in Las Vegas on December 22, 1997. I resided in an extended-stay hotel for approximately six months with an ultimate goal of purchasing my own home and establishing permanent residency. Traditionally, veterans are mobile. I was certain I wanted to reside in Las Vegas permanently. I threw caution to the wind. I needed a tax shelter. As soon as I could, I contacted the veteran's housing office and made an appointment to meet with a realtor. In a matter of weeks, I viewed multiple homes, many of which were pre-owned homes. It was a buyer's market in Las Vegas—an exceptional time to purchase a home. One of my many benefits as a veteran afforded me the opportunity to purchase a new home for a dollar down. I was exhilarated to say the least.

The Mike O'Callaghan Federal Hospital is located directly across Las Vegas Boulevard South in front of Nellis Air Force Base. Mike O'Callahan is a joint venture hospital, which means the Air Force and VA maintained joint occupancy of the hospital. My office was located on the third floor, directly across from the nurses' station on 3B medical surgical unit. There were roughly thirty inpatient beds on 3B. My colleague, Marilyn J, provided social work services to veterans admitted to 4C psychiatric unit. Four C was a fourteen-bed unit for voluntary and involuntary psychiatric admissions. Periodically, Marilyn and I covered for each other during scheduled leave or training. Today, Las Vegas has a new state-of-the art VA hospital which is located at 6900 North Pecos Drive.

My role as a social worker on 3B Medical Surgical (Med Surg) unit was not unlike my duties previously at the Aleda E. Lutz VAMC in Saginaw, Michigan. As a result of my employment experience at Aleda E. Lutz VAMC, I was efficient at conducting clinical assessments, facilitating placements in various settings, assisting veterans with completion of advance directives, and participating as a member of an interdisciplinary treatment team. Although, at Mike O'Callahan, I was required to interface with a larger volume of veterans and families. In addition, I covered surgical patients and emergency patients as needed. I remained on 3B for nearly three years. By early 2000, I decided that I needed to focus on developing my clinical skills. I was unlicensed and certain that I needed to become a Licensed Clinical Social Worker (LCSW) to enhance my eligibility for promotion. In short, I researched the requirements to become a Licensed Clinical Social Worker and began preparation for the clinical exam.

Primary Care (Ambulatory Care)

A primary care social work vacancy was posted in the Ambulatory Care Center. I spoke with the chief, Mr. D, and made him aware of my interest in the position. He encouraged me to apply for the position. I applied and was selected. While working in Ambulatory Care, it was not uncommon to interview and assess ten to fifteen veterans daily. My key responsibilities were: conducting clinical assessments, linkage of veteran and family members to VA and community resources, referral for VA compensation or pension benefits, and linkage to senior services not limited to adult protective services and advanced directives. VA social workers transfer skills and develop new skills between positions.

Many of the walk-in veteran appointments required information and referral. It remains vital for social workers to posses vast knowledge of VA and community resources. Prominent needs of veterans and families continue to be the application process for VA compensation or pension, accessing home health services (personal care assistance), widow's pensions, meals on wheels, aid and attendance, adult day health services, caregiver support, and assistance with personal expenses.

VIRGINIA A. HINES, PHD, LCSW

Veteran Service Organizations: Their Roles and Significance

A crucial connection for all VA social workers is linkage to the Veteran Service Organizations (VSO) to include: Disabled American Veterans, Purple Heart, Jewish War Veterans, American Legion, and Veterans of Foreign Wars. The significance of VSOs is that each member is a veteran. VSOs assist veterans with emergent needs to include filing new VA claims; appeals of VA claims, filing increases in service-related compensations, and submitting applications for widow's pensions. All veterans are encouraged to consider joining a VSO as these organizations are very powerful. VSOs lobby congress and fight for veteran benefits and rights.

I am partial to the Jewish War Veterans (JWVs). I was able to witness their support of veterans in action during the early part of 1998 while employed at the Mike O'Callahan Federal Hospital on 3B. A veteran on 3B Medical Surgical (Med Surg) traveled to Las Vegas and invariably gambled away his entire compensation check leaving the veteran stranded and ill in Las Vegas. The veteran contacted the local JWV and asked for assistance with an airline ticket to his destination.

Two representatives came to 3B to bring the veteran an airline ticket. I met Ed K. and one of his JWV counterparts that day. They were dressed in shirts, ties, and hats with various insignia. I inquired how I might assist them and they shared their mission to meet with a young veteran in need of airfare home. The airline ticket cost nearly $700, and JWV provided the ticket. I was pleasantly surprised to learn of the JWV and their mission. I made friends with Ed K. and his partner that day and they would later come to VA whenever I called to request assistance for veterans seeking some form of assistance (e.g., rent payment, emergency assistance when furnace malfunctions occured during the winter months, and payment of utility and telephone bills). The services the JWV and other service organizations provide to veterans is no less than phenomenal.

Behavioral Health (Psychiatry)

I remained in primary care for nearly two years. I always kept my eyes open for new and exciting opportunities to serve the veteran and enhance my skills. Eventually, there was a vacancy in general psychiatry. I applied for the position and was selected. The job required diagnosing mentally ill veterans utilizing the Diagnostic and Statistical Manual (DSM4), providing individual therapy, facilitating groups, and interfacing with families.

Immediately, I began facilitating an Anger Education Group. The group was significant as many veterans are diagnosed with Post Traumatic Stress Disorder (PTSD) and often exhibit suicidal/homicidal ideation/gestures, road rage, marital conflict, and employment challenges. The group was closed-ended and time-limited.

I utilized cognitive behavioral therapy, psycho-drama, current events, PowerPoint Presentations, and current literature (e.g., books and articles) to help veterans learn alternative thoughts, choices, and behaviors available to help them enhance their anger management skills. I interviewed each group member prior to enrolling them in the group. Individuals displaying delusions or psychotic features (auditory hallucinations, visual hallucinations, and engaging in violent behavior toward themselves or others) were not appropriate for groups and were weeded out during the initial interview process. Psychotic and delusional veterans were referred for individual therapy with the most appropriate therapist. Often, veterans are required to engage in psycho-pharmacology (psychotropic medications to manage negative behaviors and thoughts) along with individual or other forms of therapy. The VA currently uses evidence-based therapies to treat veterans coping with mental illness.

VIRGINIA A. HINES, PHD, LCSW

Women's Adjustment Group

In addition to Anger Management, I was responsible for facilitating a Women's Adjustment Group. The group met weekly and had a goal of providing a venue where women veterans could socialize, obtain support, discuss issues they faced (isolation, unemployment, relationships, compensation and pension issues), and learn about VA services. The awesome significance of groups includes, but is not limited to, attendees are privy to multiple perspectives, exposure to multiple world views, contact with individuals with diverse education levels and life experiences, normalization of problems or concerns, problem resolution, and opportunities to develop a social network. Healthy groups develop a life of their own, despite developing coalitions that may become evident during various phases of groups and challenge group facilitators.

I discovered that many women veterans had limited knowledge of compensation benefits and pension benefits or how to access them. Some women continued to struggle with issues related to having male providers (physicians) they felt were inattentive to their concerns. It is the role of social workers to be knowledgeable of compensation and pension benefits. Pension and compensation benefits are linked to monetary and concrete benefits, respectively, provided to veterans that served in military service during war periods and available to veterans injured on active duty or soldiers who had a pre-existing condition aggravated during active duty. When assisting veterans who are unaware of their benefits, a social worker's responsibility is to educate, advocate, and link veterans to benefits. Women veterans seeking assistance with resolution of provider issues are currently able to seek assistance from clinic administrators, patient advocates, or women veteran coordinators.

During my career with the VA, I have observed an escalation in the number of women veterans utilizing VA services (USDVA, 2015). As utilization of services increase, specialization in service delivery is essential to provision of quality care to VA consumers. Evidence of the evolution of the increase in services to women veterans is evidenced by the increasing number of female providers, the availability of female toiletries, female exam rooms, availability of female contraceptives, women veteran clinics at VAs nationwide, existence of research germane to women veteran issues, and the presence of women veteran coordinators at VA hospitals nationwide. A proliferation of the numbers of women veterans has spurred a proliferation of available services to women veterans (USDVA, 2017).

VIRGINIA A. HINES, PHD, LCSW

Military Sexual Trauma

Military sexual trauma (MST) treatment is a specialty area in mental health that impacts male and female soldiers. Post-traumatic stress disorder (PSTD) is historically linked to war trauma. PTSD's evolution from shell shock to hysteria and now MST exemplifies the inclusion of sexual trauma as a manifestation of PTSD. MST includes verbal communications with sexual connotations, inappropriate touching, cornering, and forced sexual contact (sexual assault against a male or female soldier) (USDVA, 2015). The contact is unwanted and therefore is a violation against the soldier.

Of interest is, at one time during my career, more men were presenting to mental health providers reporting higher incidence of MST among male soldiers than female soldiers (USDVA, 2015). The reports were both shocking and disturbing. Unfortunately, MST remains an issue impacting male and female soldiers. Educating soldiers about MST, safeguarding against MST, and reporting MST are tools used to reduce the prevalence of MST among military service members.

Relative to rating women veterans with MST, it is a rare observation for women or men veteran to be awarded total disability (100% service connected) for MST. However, in male veterans diagnosed with combat PTSD, compensation awards of 100% is common. I noted the discrepancy. I advocated for women veterans by consulting with male and female psychiatrists who were able to affect change by assisting women veterans with their applications for service-connected compensation.

I co-facilitated an MST Women Veterans' group with Mary H, a registered nurse. Mary and I kept a waiting list of women veterans interested in participating in the group. The MST group was twelve sessions in length and required participant's willingness to discuss traumatic events. To enhance my knowledge of MST, I attended the premier training program taught and administered at the Bay Pines, Florida VA Medical Center. Exposure therapy was developed and promulgated by Anna Foa as the intervention of choice to aid the treatment of MST survivors. Treatment is extended to both male and female veterans exposed to MST. I was able to witness women veterans' improvement after treatment, which was evidenced by their ability to be less suicidal, regain control of their lives by attending college, improve relationships and communication skills, and experience fewer psychiatric hospitalizations.

During training at the Bay Pines VAMC, I learned the basis of MST and the history of rape in this country. In addition, the training provided a purview of issues invaluable in aiding the trauma survivor on the road to recovery, to include identification of issues relative to coping, self-soothing activities, activities to engage in to facilitate reclaiming one's life, journaling, boundary setting (various types), statistics, trauma across the life span, subjective units of distress, anger management, and other issues.

During my training, Anna Foa published her ground-breaking book on prolonged exposure. Through the use of prolonged exposure, the trauma survivor is required to journal (write) and talk about (share) traumatic experiences multiple times. Essential to discussing trauma is safety (feeling safe and being in a safe environment and working with a therapist that is trusted) and grounding (survivor is in control and linked to the here and now so that he or she is able to stop discussing trauma at will).

Trauma survivors are encouraged to participate in treatment as soon as possible after exposure to a traumatic event and remain in treatment over the lifespan as desired. Hence, participation in psycho-pharmacology, group treatment, individual treatment, and aftercare fosters the best outcomes for trauma survivors over the lifespan.

Historically, MST survivors were required to be medically and mentally stable prior to participating in trauma treatment. Conversely, ninety days before enrolling in treatment, MST survivors could have no reported episodes of suicidal/homicidal behaviors. Other stipulations, included strict medication adherence, appointment compliance, and inclusion of a current safety plan. Currently, treatment can no longer be delayed to eligible veterans in the absence of the aforementioned stipulations.

Safety plans are required for all veterans in receipt of mental health services who have prior attempts to self-injure or commit violence against others. Veterans are required to complete their safety plans with minimal input from their mental health provider. Safety plans include a list of activities veterans usually engage in and a list of family and friends veterans will call in lieu of engaging in self-harm or aggression towards others. A copy of the safety plan is included in the veteran's treatment plan. Veterans are provided a copy of their safety plan to maintain in a place easily accessible to the veteran. Veteran are encouraged to commit to use of their safety plans. Periodically, safety plans are to be reviewed with veterans and updated to ensure continued utility.

The wars in Iraq and Afghanistan are the impetus for development of a suicide/crisis line that is functional twenty-four hours a day, seven days a week for veterans in crisis. Research revealed that calling someone listed on the safety plan may not always be feasible because the caller may not receive a response at some point. The veteran's crisis line makes it possible for veterans to speak with someone when in need of emotional support. Although, veteran suicide rates continue to rise (USDVA, 2016).

While facilitating three groups in mental health, I conducted individual therapy with veteran clients coping with various mental conditions to include, but not limited to, depression, anxiety, phobias, and psychosocial issues (employment loss, marital discord, discrimination, and financial distress). Conducting therapy was very rewarding and simultaneously draining. I learned an invaluable lesson during the seven years I worked in general psychiatry—it is imperative that mental health providers take scheduled leave to nurture themselves and revitalize in order to be fully present for veteran clients. It was during my time as a therapist that I learned I was at my best if I took quarterly leaves. Therapists that administer self-care are more likely to be fully present and supportive of clients as clients seek wellness.

Social work therapists are required to be knowledgeable of current treatment modalities and therapies. Social workers attend continuing education training in order to remain abreast of current treatments. Training and knowledge of treatment modalities facilitate development of effective treatment plans. As a mental health provider, I completed treatment plans initially, when a client's condition changed, and during scheduled intervals. Veteran clients seeking treatment are encouraged to be interested in improving their overall functioning, completing homework assignments, and showing up for scheduled appointments. Otherwise, the likelihood of change or improvement may be hampered. Treatment is a joint effort between the therapist and the client.

Addictive Disorders Treatment

In keeping with my desire to stretch, and reach my potential, I accepted an opportunity that became available to me. My employment length with VA was eleven years. Social workers were required to have a Master of Social Work degree with one year of experience. The starting grade was GS-11. For many of us, it seemed that there was a little chance of ever ascending to the GS-12 level as there were few promotional opportunities in Las Vegas. Needless to say, I learned of an opportunity in addictive disorders. The slot required clinical social work skills with vast group experience. I was more than qualified with my experience in VA to date. However, I lacked knowledge of addictions.

Growing up in a strict home with little chance to experiment with drugs and alcohol, I had fortunately limited first-hand knowledge of drug and alcohol addiction. I recognized the need to become certified in addictions. Some enticing aspects of the job included: the shift began Mondays at noon, and every other Friday was an off day. Opportunities abound in VA for employees seeking growth and promotion. Training and education facilitate various promotion opportunities.

I met with my supervisor, Pat D. and advised him of my limited knowledge of addictions. I was provided with a brochure for an addictionology certification. The requirement was that I attend a weekend class once per month for an entire year and take a test at the completion of the course. The VA paid for the training and I gladly participated. The training has served me throughout my employment and enhanced my ability to serve my patient population more effectively. The knowledge of addictions enhances the knowledge base of any healthcare professional. Drug and alcohol addiction impacts individuals, families, and organizations. Moreover, addiction crosses all settings, race, gender, and socioeconomic groups. Hence, the knowledge of addictions is another tool in the tool box of all clinicians employed in healthcare.

As an addiction therapist employed with VA, I completed initial assessments and treatment plans, facilitated groups related to addictions, participated in weekly interdisciplinary team meetings, and attended periodic continuing education training. After training, I loved to share what I learned by developing PowerPoint presentations (focused on anger and addiction, and staying clean and sober). I even constructed an addictions game (permitting group participants opportunities to win prizes for their knowledge of addictions while enhancing their knowledge of addictions). The training afforded me the opportunity to purchase current literature relative to addiction. For instance, reading, *A Million Little Pieces* by John Frey was inspirational, despite it later being publicized on the Oprah Show—the author's overzealous portrayal of his journey to recovery. I took what I could from the book and shared it with members of my groups. I loved imparting knowledge and inspiring veterans to learn about the disease of addictions, its varied causes, and current available treatments. I requested that the Jewish War Veterans participate quarterly by attending a group session to discuss their role in serving veterans and provide refreshments.

VA substance abuse programs consist of three components: pre-treatment, treatment, and aftercare. Each component is available in outpatient and inpatient settings. VA provides long-term drug, alcohol, and dual diagnosis treatment in facilities referred to as domiciliary care. Domiciles are located in various regions of the country. Domicile treatment length can range from thirty days, ninety days, one hundred eighty days, or longer based on the needs of the veteran. The requisite for domiciliary care admission is that the veteran have a treatment goal to abstain from substance use and stabilize mental health symptoms. In recent years, admission policies for domiciliary care have been enhanced. Currently, veterans cannot be denied services in the absence of prolonged abstinence. The VA continues to refine treatment that is veteran centered.

There are multiple addictions (food, drugs, alcohol, work, and sex). The theory of addiction as a disease depicts addiction as inclusive of symptoms, a determined course, treatments, prediction, and outcomes. The history of addiction relative to alcohol and other drug use is extensive, and research suggests there are three ways out of addiction: treatment, institutions (hospitals or prisons), or death. In addition, treatment is most effective when entered into by clients interested in reducing or discontinuing the use of their drug of choice. However, forced treatment is better than no treatment at all. The causes of addiction may include predisposition, abuse, and, sometimes, simple exposure to a substance. Women require less exposure time to a substance before major organ damage and death can occur when compared to their male counterparts. Often, individuals experiencing (drug) addiction also have a mental health diagnoses (referred to as dual diagnosis). A trauma of some sort may be a precursor to self-medication and drug addiction.

In this era of awareness and access to the intranet, social workers are employed in areas relative to polysubstance use, porn, cybersex, work, food, and drug addiction. Many times, individuals seeking medical treatment enter the VA with multiple addictions, so much so that clinicians are required to screen for multiple addictions and seek appropriate treatment settings for veterans.

There are aspects of addiction I was very naïve about, which include tolerance and post-acute withdrawal. Tolerance is the ability to ingest increasing amounts of a substance in order to obtain the initial effect. In other words, in order to achieve the same effect (high) as initially achieved, an individual increases the use of their substance of choice over time in order to experience the desired effect. Increased tolerance is an indication of addiction. It is not necessarily the individual we encounter falling down drunk or speaking with slurred speech that is the true addict, it is emphatically the individual known to drink or drug excessive amounts of their drug of choice that must become our major concern.

Post-acute withdrawal is a condition that occurs thirty, ninety, and up to one hundred twenty days after cessation of an addiction. Sleep is often disrupted, memory is usually negatively impacted, and re-experiencing feelings associated with active addiction are common. Addiction is a bio-psychosocial disease which requires treatments targeting biology, psychology, and psychosocial aspects of life. In other words, nutrition, exercise, structure, spirituality, mental health, and daily social aspects of life must be altered in order to treat (alter) a life disrupted by addiction. Preferred treatment environments are those mimicking, as closely as possible, the actual living environment of the individual entering treatment. It is recommended that substance abuse treatment is at a minimal of ninety to one hundred twenty days in length. Multiple treatment episodes are not uncommon. However, recovery is life-long. Individuals failing to enter treatment, change people, places, and things associated with their drug of choice, and its use may be doomed to exit addiction through death or institutions (hospitals or prisons).

The military teaches all soldiers the importance of diet and exercise. Spirituality, self-care, relationships, and coping with day-to-day living is usually taught and experienced initially in the nuclear family (home environment). Mothers or family surrogates have previously been tasked with teaching self-care and social skills to children. Too often, individuals in active addiction lack family or social supports due to negative consequences related to addictive behaviors (e.g., incarceration, legal issues, impulsive decisions, and the absence of income). The twelve-step programs along with sponsorship serve as social supports that facilitate relationship building during recovery.

Aftercare is essential to long-term recovery and is often ignored, devalued, or neglected by individuals lacking full understanding of addictions and the lifelong road to recovery. Participation in aftercare seems illogical to someone who has never lived clean and sober from the use of addictive substances. A female veteran once inquired, "How long will it take me to recover from cocaine addiction?" I noted her recent weight loss and applauded her efforts. The female veteran was a federal employee who shared that her weight loss was attributed to frequent cocaine use. The employee was aware of my position in the Addictive Disorders Treatment Program (ADTP). The employee inquired if there was a local program she might enroll. The employee was encouraged to consider attending the treatment program available at our clinic. However, confidentiality was a concern that deterred the employee from entering treatment. When the employee learned that recovery was a lifelong process that often involved relapse, she began crying. Many become involved with substance use without knowledge of long-term ramifications of substance use relative to health and other aspects of life. Employee assistance programs are essential to the maintenance of an addiction free workforce.

While employed as an addiction therapist, I discovered that many veteran participating in treatment were unaware of the necessity to participate in a ninety to one hundred twenty-day treatment program at a minimum before they could be considered clean and sober. Cessation of substance use and failure to complete an addiction program is descriptive of being dry. In other words, the use of a drug of choice is active addiction despite periodic cessation of use of a substance of choice.

While attending a conference that addressed trauma and recovery, I discovered an exceptional book and workbook entitled *Staying Clean and Sober*, written and illustrated by Dr. David Smith. The workbook illustrated the ideal of maintenance as it relates to individuals who were not in active addiction and provided daily and weekly activities to be completed by the recovering individual in order for the individual to live clean and sober.

Individuals in recovery require examples of individuals living clean and sober to facilitate transition from active addiction to sobriety. The importance of the twelve-step groups are the inherent social support and role modeling exemplified during participation in the twelve-step groups.

Previous schools of thought suggested that the best example of recovery was someone previously addicted to the same substance that transitioned to sober living. However, today, examples of clean and sober living are not limited to those in recovery. People who have never abused drugs or alcohol may serve as effective role models for those transitioning from active addiction to clean and sober living.

The repercussions of drug (includes alcohol) addiction are vast at both the micro-level and macro-levels of society. At the micro-level, individual loss is manifested through destruction of families, employment loss, personal injuries, and legal problems resulting from years of entanglement with the criminal justice system. Micro-level challenges includes attempts to resolve or recover from health issues stemming from chronic drug, alcohol, and other addictions. Conversely, at the macro-level, societal compromise is unparalleled as a result of drug and alcohol addiction. Companies experience millions of dollars in lost productivity due to call-ins for un-scheduled sick leave, loss resulting from damage to equipment by employees under the influence of substances, and the loss of life emanating from fatalities linked to drunk or buzzed driving.

Some substance abusers never ascend to restoration as when there is evidence of addictions because substantial collateral damage is not uncommon. I learned to listen more and allow individuals presenting for treatment to decide when they were ready for treatment. Most of all, I witnessed veterans reclaiming their lives and becoming productive members of society. To date, it is not a requisite for the therapist to have dual roles—one role signifying recovery and the other signifying counselor or therapist. Any educated individual living clean and sober may serve as an effective role model for individuals in recovery.

I had an experience that started on an inpatient medicine unit—transitioned to the intensive care unit and invariably, each unit I have been privileged to work on at VA. It is the story of addiction. A veteran was admitted to the Medicine Unit at Aleda E. Lutz VA so often I memorized his social security number. One day, I inquired of the veteran his reason for refusing treatment for alcohol addiction so that he might stop drinking and alleviate the need for multiple successive re-admissions to the Medicine Unit. The veteran indicated that he would never stop drinking. He didn't, and he eventually died due to complications from alcohol addiction. Perhaps the veteran was unable to stop drinking on his own and was disinterested in any of the viable options available at VA to facilitate sobriety. Treatment requires participant involvement. VA has an array of inpatient, outpatient, and long-term treatment options available to service members and veterans seeking sobriety.

Significant Lessons Learned

- *Both the Department of Veteran Affairs and the U.S. military are institutions that facilitate personal growth and development.*
- *In whatever phase of life we are in, we can still learn.*
- *Never be afraid to embrace new challenges in life.*
- *We have a duty to empower ourselves and those we encounter that require assistance.*
- *We are limited if we think we are limited.*
- *Addiction continues to impact micro and macro levels of our society.*
- *Knowledge of addiction and its ramifications are essential to all members of society.*
- *Treatment of addiction usually encompasses inpatient or outpatient services.*
- *Components of addiction treatment usually entail pre-treatment, treatment, and aftercare.*
- *Recovery from addictive substances is lifelong!*

> *A chance encounter sparks a trajectory of adventure, growth, and development, which take on their own momentum. A chance encounter sparks a trajectory of adventure, growth, and development, which take on their own momentum. A chance encounter sparks a trajectory of adventure, growth, and development, which take on their own momentum. Take it on! Take it on! Take it on! Stop playing it safe! Stop playing it safe! Stop playing it safe!*

CHAPTER 7

DISSERTATION: VIRGINIA A. HINES, PHD, LCSW

In January 2003, I had an interesting conversation with a nurse I met while completing a training in San Diego, California. Aurora M. was one of the smartest women I met in VA. She was a registered nurse (RN) and a female veteran completing a doctorate (PhD) degree in Business. I fantasized about completing a doctorate degree in 1995. I discovered an African-American woman with a PhD in Psychology in Detroit, Michigan. Because of my curiosity about her daily tasks and how she interacted with clients, I decided to arrange an interview with her. I was so impressed by the woman, I applied for admission to a PhD program at a small university in Detroit. However, I was not selected for admission. I set the ideal of obtaining a PhD aside for a while. But somehow, I always felt I would return to college for a doctorate.

Interestingly, many years later, a nurse would encourage me to consider returning to college to begin studies for my PhD. Is it interesting or is it destiny? It is the latter. Similarly, I met a social worker, Michelle L., who was also working on a PhD. Michelle encouraged me to consider returning to college to obtain a PhD. She was enrolled at Capella University—an online university located in Minneapolis, Minnesota. Enrolling in online courses was appealing as I would be able to continue to work full-time and complete my course work at my own pace. I was apprehensive about the validity and respectability of Capella University and online learning. I researched the school to find out about the ratio of professors to students, graduation rates, supportive services, and, of course, cost. I discovered that more and more individuals were pursuing online learning due to their schedules. Flexibility of schedules and increased enrollments indicated some level of acceptability from respective employers for hiring Capella graduates. Capella required three weeks of residency, so there was a brick-and-mortar component. Also, the course work was rigorous, which is indicative of an attrition rate. Capella assigned mediators to each student. Mediators were responsible for tracking student progress and assisting students with challenging issues or concerns. I investigated the transferability of my Master's Degree level courses from the University of Maryland to Capella's curriculum and degree programs. Needless to say, Capella's staff were flexible and worked to attract and maintain students in their programs with appealing graduation rates.

I decided to enroll in an online course to test my ability to matriculate through the computer programs and test the feasibility of continuing full-time employment. Needless to say, I was hooked after completing my first course. While working in addictions at VA during the day, completing my Addictionology certificate one weekend per month, and taking online courses, I worked towards the completion of a PhD in Human Services. Undertaking the course work for a PhD while working full-time and obtaining an Addiction certificate were the most challenging tasks of my life. I completed my PhD studies in September 2009. I would be remiss if I did not highlight the experience, but delving too deeply into the experience would be the foundation of a second book.

It is essential that doctoral degrees are undertaken as personal challenges to those in pursuit of a PhD. Questions relative to the purpose for obtaining the PhD would be useful to address prior to beginning a PhD program and identify a goal to help the learner remain focused pursuant to her goal. I have never begun a journey without considering the purpose and goal of my journey. I do not imagine I would have been able to handle the taunting, demeaning, and outright hazing that I was subjected to by my initial dissertation chair had I not understood my goal to complete the program. Quitting was never an option for me. I have never quit anything in my life. Important issues to be addressed by doctoral candidates include availability of a reliable support network, commitment to the process, a schedule that is followed rigorously, establishment of connections with other doctoral candidates, and linkage to individuals who have already obtained PhDs in their field of choice to serve as mentors.

A strong support network is essential to a PhD candidate as the candidate will require a great deal of encouragement, especially during times the endeavor becomes taxing and the candidate has pause to renege on pursuit of the PhD. The support network must appreciate the goal and serve as a buffer for stress and other distractions threatening to derail the pursuit of the PhD. Additionally, the support network must be instrumental in encouraging the PhD candidate to rest or take periodic hiatus.

Finally, the support network must provide encouragement to the candidate on days when dreams of obtaining a PhD are dashed by other life crisis. Supports provide reminders of the importance of self-soothing because candidates need to be very focused, at times relentless, and unwilling to take their eyes off the prize. Candidates who lose focus or take their eyes off the prize even for a second could resolve to never resume the pursuit of their PhD. Throughout the process, support networks iterate time and again the belief that the PhD candidate is capable of obtaining a PhD.

Achieving any great challenge can never be undertaken in isolation. When winners have been questioned about the greatest asset facilitating the attainment of their PhD (or some other great quest), winners attested to an inability to ascend to the highest pinnacle in their lives in the absence of family and friends. In other words, the winner credited her support system (inclusive of God).

Commitment is essential to any task undertaken. Prior to embarking upon my PhD in 2003, I imagined that Basic and Advanced Training in the U.S. Army were the most challenging undertakings of my life. I was in for a surprise. It is awesome to inform others when we are doing something great. However, actually enduring until the end and achieving goals we have shared with others is the ultimate satisfaction. Multiple people asked how things were going as I pursued my PhD, but few imagined the vast amount of work and the long hours required to achieve such an undertaking. Many PhD candidates start their programs, but few obtain the degree. Many candidates talk about what they are going to do and never take one step towards attaining their goal. Conversely, others attain their goals and go on to attain additional goals. Success is a requisite of mastery. Success emphatically triggers additional success, and the best predictor of future success is previous success, which is mastery.

What gets in the way of goal attainment (completing the PhD)? Life. Life happens to us in spite of our goals. Family and loved ones leave you because you study too much. Some significant others believe once you obtain a PhD, you will leave them, so they leave you. People die. Babies are born. Individuals close to you become ill. Your integrity is questioned and people inquire, "Why do you want a PhD? You won't make more money." How absurd. Not every goal undertaken is linked to financial gain, at least not initially. I was shocked at the candor and rudeness of some individuals.

I was horrified to learn the number of individuals that begin but never complete doctoral degrees yet proudly flaunt, "I am ABD (*all but dissertation*)." I never spoke or wanted others to say those words to me. How sad to almost achieve a goal. There is no such thing as almost achieving. You either do or do not achieve your goals.

When challenged by goals, obstacles, or foes, the dreamer becomes a candidate with real intent and never relents. The candidate will finish. Through commitment to the task, touching (working on) it daily, incrementally (researching articles, discussing it with my support network, and lying in bed with my dissertation) my dissertation became an extension of who I am and eventually a dream come true. Glory to God!

My schedule included full-time employment (forty hours) Monday through Friday, coming home, eating and grooming myself, taking a nap, getting up at 9 PM, and studying until the wee hours; only to go to work and begin the entire process over again the next day. Weekends were my best time because I was able to sleep in and go to the gym, grocery store, and the University of Las Vegas library where I studied for six hours on Saturdays. On Sundays, I attended church when possible, cooked for the week, and worked on my dissertation. Occasionally, I took a break to listen to jazz, go dancing (stepping), and take in a movie. The library became my second home. I met Carol S., a librarian, who became a great friend and support. She assisted me with my research efforts and I, in turn, served as an encourager to Carol S. as she worked to complete a self-help book. God facilitates divine connections. In our time of need, God dispatches angels to take care of his children. Thank you Lord!

If I had not gone to step class, I would never have met Debra D., a school principal with a PhD in Education. Debra D. agreed to read my dissertation. She linked me to another individual who agreed to serve as an editor. While completing our tasks or while on our path (grinding), we meet people who are positive, creative, and supportive of our endeavor because they are achievers (grinders). However, I had to remain rigid or structured in my routine as I feared that the loss of structure may have become an excuse for failure to complete my goal. God knows what we need and delivers on time. I reflect on my journey and use it to fuel my efforts to complete this book and other projects (grinds) I am working on. Mastery solidifies additional mastery. God makes the impossible possible. Grind baby, grind!

I have always enjoyed reading books. I knew immediately the course work for any doctorate degree would require research. Research is usually conducted at a library (online library and intranet). I recall

ON BECOMING AN INDIVIDUAL, A SOLDIER, A PROFESSIONAL LICENSED CLINICAL SOCIAL WORKER

contacting Michelle L. to suggest that we meet at the University of Las Vegas library, as I had to begin research for a writing assignment. Michelle responded, "I am not feeling that. I do not feel like writing any papers. I am not going to be taking any more classes." I had a flashback to my preparation for the Army. I had thoughts of my three classmates who were supposed to accompany me to the Army but were unable to go with me for various reasons. I was the only one to enter the Army at that time. There I was again…the only one. Do I persevere or do I give up? Obtaining a doctoral degree was my goal, just as entering the Army had been. I owned my goal to obtain a PhD and remained on task. I would not be denied or deterred. Less than one percent of the U.S. population hold a doctoral degree. The percentage of African-Americans pursuing and completing PhDs is less than one percent.

While attending my initial onsite colloquia with Capella University, I met Dr. Shirley J. and Dr. Sandra B. Students at Capella were required to complete three weeks of onsite colloquia, which provided opportunities for students and faculty to interface. Dr. Shirley enrolled in Capella prior to Dr. Sandra and me. Dr. Shirley was our leader and kept us inspired to complete our PhD. Dr. Sandra enrolled at Capella and completed several courses over a period of time prior to committing to her PhD program. We clicked immediately and vowed to remain in touch and anchor each other through the matriculation of our programs.

Dr. Shirley insisted upon visiting me in Las Vegas. It was a nice reunion. I maintained contact with Dr. Sandra often. During a visit to Jacksonville, Florida, to visit Dr. Shirley, I learned about the acceptance of her dissertation. Dr. Shirley agreed to review my dissertation and provide invaluable feedback. Dr. Shirley obtained her PhD in Education. I obtained my PhD in Human Services, and Dr. Sandra obtained her PhD in Counseling. My dissertation topic is "Homelessness: Women Veterans' Perspective." I continue to receive royalty checks for the sale of my dissertation…Glory to God! My dissertation consisted of a qualitative study of several homeless women veteran encountered in Las Vegas, Nevada. Do you think you know what contributes to homelessness among women veteran? Read my dissertation and enhance your knowledge.

Significant Lessons Learned

- *If you have a desire to take on a task, seek God's guidance first. Then go after the task with tenacity. God is faithful and he will come through. God will never allow us to fail at the desires he has painted on the canvas of our hearts! (Joel Osteen)*
- *If obtaining a PhD were easy, everyone would have one…*
- *Don't ever allow life circumstances to pre-empt goal attainment…crisis do not last forever. Rest if you must, but don't you quit!*
- *Keep taking risks!*
- *Always reach back to help someone along their way. Stay connected to wholesomeness…to God!*

Doctorate of Philosophy in Human Services. Capella University. 2009. Virginia A. Hines, PhD.

> *Become a lifelong learner. Challenge yourself to become the best that you can be! Become a lifelong learner. Challenge yourself to become the best that you can be! Become a lifelong learner. Challenge yourself to become the best that you can be! Define success by achieving all that you set out to achieve. Define success by achieving all that you set out to achieve. Define success by achieving all that you set out to achieve!*

CHAPTER 8

HEALTH CARE FOR RE-ENTRY VETERANS

On September 30, 2009 I was notified of the acceptance of my dissertation and its approximate publication date. I was ecstatic. Simultaneously I was celebrating nineteen years of employment with the Department of Veteran Affairs. Because of my success, I began to seek opportunities for advancement. However, VA social workers were not considered a critical profession, resulting in no financial assistance with payment for my doctorate. Unlike the nurses, I was required to shoulder the entire cost of my doctorate. I was not happy about this discourse, but decided to persevere.

I was employed with the ADTP several more months before seeking other employment opportunities. VA continues to grow and expand service delivery to meet the changing needs of the veterans. Research focusing on incarcerated veteran was underway. A vacancy occurred requiring outreach to state and federal prisons to facilitate the reintegration of incarcerated veterans to the VA and society. There was a supposition that many incarcerated veterans were eligible for VA benefits but had never accessed VA services. The VA extended benefits to eligible incarcerated veteran.

In view of my previous experience as a military police officer (six years) and employment in a woman's corrections facility, I was unafraid of entering prisons and federal halfway houses to render service to veterans. I was provided a new government car, two travel cards (hotel and gas), and autonomy to fulfill the obligations of the position. VA social workers are entrusted with various levels of autonomy and responsibility. Service to veterans is our top priority.

The opportunity to develop the Health Care for Re-Entry Veteran Program was exciting. I conducted a literature review; identified each local, state, and federal penal institution in Southern Nevada; established contact with a VA counterpart located in California, who allowed me to shadow him while he conducted outreach at his assigned prisons; developed an Excel Database to document each veteran encounter; established progress notes in the VA patient electronic record with the assistance of the Coding staff; Developed a PowerPoint presentation; and contacted the state director of the Department of Corrections to request a meeting. The PowerPoint presentation outlined the VA mission, goals, and objectives in integrating re-entry veteran into the VA healthcare system.

In short, the re-entry veteran are impacted by a range of health maladies to include, but not limited to, hepatitis C, HIV, addiction, and homelessness. If left unchecked, the aforementioned maladies would invariably infiltrate the re-entry veteran, their families, and their communities; contribute to higher healthcare costs, and wreak havoc on state, local, and federal budgets. Veteran families, communities, and society benefit when services are provided to special populations of veterans.

Addiction and homelessness, in turn, contribute to higher rates of crime and recidivism. The issue of homeless veterans continue to be a significant topic in the media. The previous Secretary of the Department of Veteran Affairs, Erick Shinseki, and President Obama pledged to end homelessness among veterans by 2015 (USDVA, 2017). Research revealed that many veterans exiting the criminal justice system experienced homelessness upon release and often engaged in criminal activities to ensure re-incarceration in order to obtain shelter. The VA's continued efforts to engage the re-entry veteran is necessary but was met with initial resistance by some stakeholders.

The PowerPoint presentation that I developed overviewed the VA's role in serving re-entry veterans and was utilized to educate internal and external stakeholders. A work group and several volunteer mentors were instrumental in developing a brochure that outlined the services that were administered to the re-entry veterans. The brochure was widely dispersed. I wrote an article outlining the VA's role in service delivery to re-entry veterans that was published in the National Association of Social Worker's Health Administration Newsletter. The PowerPoint presentation was instrumental in facilitating my admission to nineteen state and federal prisons and halfway houses in the Southern Nevada Catchment area.

I traveled to each facility monthly, conducted presentations to groups of veteran inmates, and assisted them with acquiring their DD214 (military discharge papers). I worked with veterans to develop viable release plans predicated upon successful re-entry into society. Release plans explored housing options, employment interests, relationships, clothing, healthcare needs, community services, reinstatement of VA compensations, and substance abuse treatment.

Not all veteran inmates were successful with re-entry. From 2009 to 2011, I served as a re-entry specialist. I assessed more than a thousand veterans and witnessed a less than one percent recidivism rate among those assessed. I learned of gaps in services available to re-entry veterans, to include: limited interviewing skills, anger issues, and lack of social supports. To mediate gaps in services to re-entry veteran, I recruited community volunteers and those sympathetic to veteran issues. With the assistance of community volunteers, an aftercare group was developed. The group sessions addressed topics that represented gaps in services to re-entry veterans.

I met with re-entry veterans' family members and a few veteran service organizations (The Jewish War Veterans and Disabled American Veteran) to discuss the needs of re-entry veterans and garner support. In support of all veterans, the Veteran Health Administration is an integrated healthcare system that provides services to veterans in greater than 1,400 diverse locations. As the needs of the veterans evolve, the range of services evolve to meet their needs.

Significant Lessons Learned

- *Greatness costs effort, time, money, and sometimes relationships.*
- *Remain open to possibilities.*
- *Never quit anything of substantive value to you!*
- *Never gauge your success on someone else's standards.*
- *Love shows up and shows out.*
- *God dispatches angels to help us, often at our lowest point or when facing a grave challenge. You will make it...*
- *VA is synonymous to a transformer that morphs new dimensions as it evolves and mitigates the needs of soldiers, veterans, and family caregivers.*

> *Transition is synonymous with change. Transition is synonymous with change. Transition is synonymous with change. We are always evolving, looking forward, looking back! We are always evolving, looking forward, looking back! We are always evolving, looking forward, looking back! Thrive in the midst of discomfort and uncertainty! Thrive in the midst of discomfort and uncertainty! Thrive in the midst of discomfort and uncertainty!*

CHAPTER 9

SOCIAL WORK SERVICE CHIEF

After two years of employment as a re-entry specialist, I recognized a need to grow and stretch into a new role. Promotions were virtually unheard of among VA social workers. In fact, the social work position description had not been reviewed or updated in more than forty-two years. The social work service chief position was just about the only position in VA that I had not been employed. With my PhD in Human Services and a certificate in Leadership, I was certain there was nothing I could not do or learn. I discussed my decision with my support network and received affirming responses. The decision to seek another position was bittersweet as I was entrenched in Las Vegas after 14 years. I had friends and activities that I engaged regularly. Yet the Army's mantra, "Be all you can be," spurred me to continue to stretch (grow) professionally and accept new challenges.

Promotions are not readily accessible unless you are mobile. Historically, I check things out prior to relocating. It was comforting that all my time and leave with VA would transfer with me wherever I moved as long as I remained a federal employee (another benefit).

I started looking for promotion opportunities while pursuing my PhD. For two consecutive years, I noticed a continuous vacancy in Big Spring, Texas, seeking a Chief of Social Work. I would later learn about the challenges in hiring and maintaining quality employees in a remote rural setting such as West Texas. I decided to apply for the position. The interview went well. I decided to take a trip to Big Spring once I accepted the position. It was a small oil-rich part of the country, a Bush territory. The town seemed dilapidated initially, however, there were several nice locations that made me feel certain the move would be a positive endeavor. I met with a realtor in Big Spring who took me to view several properties. I actually found a house I really liked. However, because of my ambivalence about selling my home in Las Vegas and uncertainty about remaining in Big Spring for the long haul, I decided to rent a place to live. Long ago I learned that material things can be replaced but my happiness is paramount. I could purchase another home at a later date. But at the time, I concluded that it was too soon to make a decision about another major purchase, such as a new home.

During my visit to Big Spring, I did not visit the VA. I was certain that I would be able to handle whatever awaited me. I decided to take the job. It was an $8,000 increase and a grade 13. After my arrival, I learned that someone looked me up on the Intranet and spread a rumor that I was a middle aged, Caucasian female moving to Big Spring to retire. When I reported to work on December 4, 2011, the whispering began. People were shocked to learn that the information gleaned from the rumor mill was not legitimate. I was surprised to later learn of the rumor and was admittedly hurt. I did not report the rumor. However, it was the beginning of the challenges I would endure as the Chief of Social Work Service at the West Texas VA.

As a service chief, I tried to focus on the direction I wanted to take the staff, but I had many lessons to learn about leadership despite my certificate in leadership. I received a lot of support from the medical center director, other service chiefs, and some female veterans on staff. While chief, I was able to lead the staff to exceed and meet key performance measures never previously attained. I awarded hard work with performance awards. The great part of being a service chief included the opportunity to gain experience with budgeting (flow at a medical center), defending my service level budget to the medical center director, participating in the hiring process, learning the role of human resources, administrating a service line, and, most of all, the challenging demands of people management. I was fortunate to be mentored by one of the greatest social workers I ever met, Pete S. With his assistance, creative ideas were formulated into plans to eradicate open referrals and meet performance measures in turn.

After nearly two years of doing the best job I could in spite of a myriad of obstacles, I decided it was time to take care of myself. Working overtime daily and most weekends, completing tasks with limited staff, coping with administrative challenges, adjusting to multiple levels of administration, and identifying areas that were threats to the service level budget was very demanding. I spent many hours going back and forth to Human Resources, documenting performance and obtaining guidance. In short, I needed a change and determined I was best at program management. I began to look for and was successful in finding another meaningful position as a VA liaison which provided me the opportunity to incorporate many of the principles that I have learned to date as a VA social worker.

Significant Lessons Learned

- *The higher your position, the greater the requirement to put yourself last.*
- *Greatness is not measured by the height of my position or pay grade but in my ability to serve him/her who has borne the battle.*
- *I decide when enough is enough. It is okay to change directions.*
- *Once I realize that I am in a mistake, I correct it. Do not hang on hoping things will improve. Often, the situation will only continue to deteriorate.*
- *Make improvements wherever you go. Accomplishments belong to the achiever, not the observer or critic.*
- *Hurt people seek to hurt or destroy other people. Don't be a victim.*

> *Whatever your vocation of choice, do it to the glory and honor of God! Whatever your vocation of choice, do it to the glory and honor of God! Whatever your vocation of choice, do it to the glory and honor of God! Keep on reaching for the sky! Keep on reaching for the sky! Keep on reaching for the sky!*

CHAPTER 10

Veterans Administration (VA) Liaison for Healthcare

When considering the opportunity to transition into another position, I wanted a position that would integrate many of my previous work experiences. The VA liaison position incorporated many of my previous social work tasks. As a VA liaison for healthcare I utilized multiple VA programs to document clinical assessments and track soldiers transferring from military treatment facilities to VA hospitals nationwide. As a VA liaison, I received military treatment referrals from U.S. Army nurse case managers, scheduled and conducted clinical assessments with each soldier departing the Army base due to medical discharge, identified high-risk soldiers for priority services, highlighted required services for soldiers to receive at their destination VA, and provided the service member with the address of the closest VA medical center to their destination address. Emergency points of contact at the receiving VA were provided to the service member. All transitioning soldiers were provided an overview of VA benefits and services. I was responsible for tracking referrals until appointments for care were established at the VA and authorizations for early medical care were received.

The VA Liaison for Healthcare position required constant communication between the VA social worker and the Army nurse case managers in order to ensure timely linkage of service members to VA services. I facilitated a weekly briefing with transitioning service members to education them about my role as a VA liaison and to iterate the importance of our meeting prior to them departing the military treatment facility. Service members were educated about my role as a VA liaison and encouraged to meet with me prior to departing the base.

The VA liaison position aluminates multiple skill sets critical to the role of VA social workers (e.g. advocacy during interdisciplinary team meetings on behalf of service members, identification of pre and post discharge needs for service members, the sharing of knowledge relative to unique VA services available to transitioning service members, and the best way to access services).

The Foreign Medical Program provides healthcare services to service men and women who live and work overseas after discharge from military service. The program permits service men and women with service-related injuries to select medical providers overseas. The VA liaison provided an overview of services and benefits of the Foreign Medical Program to all service members electing to work and live overseas after being medically discharged from military service.

I was instrumental in maintaining a level of performance for five consecutive years that resulted in payment of millions of reimbursement dollars to the VA. In short, when service members departed the military installation with established appointments, I demonstrate effective programming and service delivery to soldiers and their families.

In this current climate of war and constant threats against America and its allies, it is essential that VA social workers are skilled and versatile in their ability to deliver quality services to our nation's veterans. Clinical social workers are essential in the treatment of soldiers, veterans, and family caregivers.

VIRGINIA A. HINES, PHD, LCSW

Significant Lessons Learned

- *Each professional utilizes specific tools in the execution of their craft; the clinical assessment is my tool.*
- *Excellence is exemplified by exceeding expectations.*
- *U.S. Soldiers and Veterans deserve the best care possible.*
- *VA continues to develop and refine service delivery to our nation's soldiers, veterans and caregivers.*

> *Systems*
>
> *Are goal-directed, integrated, consist of multiple parts, unable to function at their optimal in the absence of communication, take stock of their environment, make adjustments as warranted, forge new service sectors, conduct ongoing evaluation analysis, and utilize best practices. Hence, The Veterans Health Administration...*

CHAPTER 11

Systems: Veterans Health Administration (Program Highlights)

The Veterans Health Administration has, since the wars in Iraq and Afghanistan, developed additional programs to include, but not limited to, Caregiver Support, Veterans' Crises Line, MyHealtheVet, Women Veteran's Coordinator, and HUDVASH.

VIRGINIA A. HINES, PHD, LCSW

Program Highlights

The Caregiver Support Program is the first of its kind in the nation where clinical requirements exist; authorize a spouse, adult family member, or significant other to provide twenty-four-hour in-home care to a veteran. The Department of Veteran Affairs pays the caregiver a monthly stipend and provides respite hours which permit the caregiver time to address their individual medical care and leisure activities. During the caregiver's respite, a back-up caregiver from a Joint Commission-approved agency is in the home to provide supportive care to the service member or veteran. The Caregiver Support program is not a benefit. It is provided to eligible service members or veterans requiring clinical services (USDVA, 2015).

In response to the historic suicide rate of twenty veterans per day, the Department of Veteran Affairs implemented the Veterans' Crisis Line (twenty-four hours a day, seven days per week) (USDVA, 2016). The hotline (crisis line) is not only available to service members or veterans contemplating suicide or homicide, but any service member or veteran in need of someone to speak to relative to stressors may call the crisis line. Callers articulating a plan with intent to engage in self-harm or homicide are asked to go to the nearest emergency room. If the service member or veteran refuses, emergency medical technicians and authorities are dispatched to the residence to escort the service member to the hospital. Anyone wishing to contact the Veterans' Crisis Line may call 800-273-8255 (USDVA, 2016).

Have you ever witnessed healthcare at your fingertips? MyHealtheVet is a web-based program accessible via the VA.gov website. Several actions can be performed from a home computer or IPhone which allow the service member to (a) communicate with their healthcare provider (Monday to Friday from 8 AM to 4:30 PM); (b) request medication refills, which are mailed out to the SM or veteran and received usually within three to five business days; (c) review lab work and print a copy of the report; (d) instant message the provider or nurse to request a same-day appointment and or move a scheduled appointment to a preferred time; (e) review progress notes previously completed by a provider and print them; and (f) manage personal healthcare by maintaining an online journal and more. To access MyHealtheVet, a user name and passcode are required. There is a MyHealtheVet coordinator at each VA medical center who will assist service members or veterans as warranted (USDVA, 2016).

Despite historic efforts, homelessness continues to plague our nation's veterans. The VA has always maintained programs to address homelessness. However, in 2009, President Obama and the Secretary of the Department of Veteran Affairs, Erick Shinseki, vowed to eradicate homelessness among veterans. A program that elicits joint efforts from the U.S. Department of Housing and Urban Development (HUD) and the VA Supportive Housing Program (VASH) is commonly referred to as HUDVASH.

The HUD dispersed housing vouchers to VA's nationwide based on homeless point in time reports in an effort to house homeless veterans. What is so awesome about the program is that there is a call center that homeless veterans can call to leave their contact information and current housing needs. The call center staff sends the information on the lines to the nearest VA, and the VA supportive Housing Specialist contacts the veteran to arrange a face-to-face interview. HUDVASH is income based, and applicants must be literally homeless or at risk of becoming homeless. Once eligibility is confirmed, service members and veterans are able to view houses or apartments and even select their preference. Individuals with income pay a sliding scale for rent. Placement is usually utilized until the veteran or service member becomes self-supporting (USDVA, 2017).

Another program that was inspired through the wars in Iraq and Afghanistan is the Women Veteran Coordinator. We had more women than ever before serving during these wars, and services have been improved for women veteran as a result. There is a women veteran coordinator at all VAs nationwide. The coordinator has vast responsibilities to include, but not limited to, mediating issues facing women veteran; conducting outreach to women veterans, and providing information, referrals, and conducting analysis relative to issues facing women Veteran (USDVA, 2017). There is a Women's Veteran Health Clinic at each VA that is staffed by all female providers.

Each of the aforementioned programs are usually managed or coordinated by a masters prepared licensed clinical or independent social worker. Please view www.socialwork.va.gov for a more exhaustive overview of the myriad social work services available at VA's nationwide. usajobs.gov provides current federal vacancies for Social Workers.

Significant Lessons Learned

- *Healthcare services at VAs nationwide have been expanded to provide more comprehensive healthcare services to women veterans.*
- *I am great at what I do. My experience is VAST!*
- *No matter how others perform, always bring your A game to work!*
- *My God is all mighty! He watches over me and he is a rewarder of all deeds.*
- *Love what you get paid to do as most of your day is spent within its confines…*
- *When one grind ends, another one begins…*

Conclusion

I had several goals in mind as I chronicled my experiences. First, I wanted to highlight the role of parents in effecting growth, developing risk-taking behavior and self-reliance in their children. Great parenting aids children in developing fulfilling lives. Second, it was my desire to highlight the U.S. Army and its role in helping me to pay attention to detail, meet challenges, bolster my career development, and learn of the many benefits available to soldiers who serve this country. Third, I wanted to reveal how I took risks from an early age by joining the military and highlight my transition from high school to the Army, from the Army to college, and from college into my current career in Federal Service. Participating in secondary and post-graduate education is challenging. College may not be of interest to young people struggling to complete high school. But the U.S. military can be a conduit to a rewarding career for individuals willing to work hard. The military provides opportunities for education, travel, and career development.

I was fortunate to serve in the U.S. Army, as the Army afforded me an opportunity to achieve my initial goal of attending college. Young people need to be aware of a myriad of ways to achieve their educational goals. Life is not without challenges. Some people are able to set goals and attain them with ease. Others struggle to find ways to create the life they desire. Individuals who are able to recognize opportunities and take advantage of them have great potential to become winners in life. Individuals who are able to follow their dreams become self-actualized and have a great propensity to later contribute to the growth and development of others. No life is without challenges. It is much easier to remain committed to goals you establish rather than goals or commitments imposed upon you by others. So, dream big! Do not limit God or yourself.

Fourth, I wanted to illustrate how connections or friendships made during junior high and high school have the potential to steer young people away from or solidify their current goals. My experiences highlighted my willingness to persevere alone after high school despite the early alteration in the plans of my classmates. The youth are encouraged to be cognizant of their associations in life. Friends and associates are diverse terms. The youth are encouraged to develop relationships with positive people who are engaging in positive activities, subsequently, fostering positive energy and proliferating success. When family or friends are unable to meet their obligations, it does not signal giving up on personal goals. In many instances, it is essential that we create our own paths and go our own way to attain personal success.

Fifth, I grew up during an era in which marijuana was the most popular drug for recreational or experimental use. Marijuana was hailed as none habit-forming and harmless. Through my education and employment opportunities, I learned about the ramifications of drug use (includes alcohol). Contrary to what we believed, substance abuse generally has negative outcomes. Historically, the youth are socialized around addictive substances. In turn, substance use disorders plague lives, communities, and society. Leading a spiritual life full of activities that promote health, learning and fun are the crux of a quality life and wellbeing.

Sixth, this book illuminates how I found my niche early in life. The youth are encouraged to investigate education and career opportunities that peak their interests. The parents are encouraged to consider my mother's decision to allow me to make my own decisions relative to my education and military career choices. Note her sacrifice…parents can empower their children for life by allowing their children to make small decisions initially. But as children mature, their opportunities for making more significant decisions should expand into adulthood. As a result, generations of children will enter adulthood and feel good about entering careers or training they enjoy. Making mistakes is a part of life. But learning to trust yourself is important and essential to becoming an adult.

Seventh, while transitioning into adulthood, serving in the military, attending graduate school, selecting social work as a career path, and participating in post-secondary education are included in this chronicle of my segway to personal success, it is my prayer that this chronicle will serve as a light to someone struggling to become their best self by walking into their God-given destiny (grind)!

ON BECOMING AN INDIVIDUAL, A SOLDIER, A PROFESSIONAL LICENSED CLINICAL SOCIAL WORKER

Employment in a federal system that affords great benefits to include, but not limited to, paid annual leave, paid sick leave, family leave; health insurance; the ability to purchase military time served and add it to civil service retirement; accumulating a thirty-two plus year retirement (for me) is possible! Are there better systems? Perhaps. The beauty of America is the freedom to choose where we work and often influence our hours. The U.S. Army (military) creates a platform of learning, traveling, and obtaining benefits that can be actualized if individuals transition from the U.S. Military into the civil service employment force. Are there risks involved? Sure, but there are risks if we do not select employment that is stable and enjoyable.

I have been fortunate to work in thirteen or more different positions inclusive of the U.S. Army. I am blessed and fortunate to serve those who have served this great nation. No job is always luxurious. Each day we are faced with challenges in a changing world. Planning, making tough choices, saving money, and staying on course pays off. If you are not certain where you are going and need a challenge, consider becoming all you can be by joining the military and or seeking federal employment. We cannot allow threats of war or danger to detour us. We are not immune to threats against our safety at home, work, or play. Risk it all. Whether you retire from the military, work in civil service, or both, you cannot go wrong when serving your country. Take a chance…get started. Grind baby, grind!

> *GRIND is a euphemism for goal/plan/dream. It's near and dear to your heart. Perhaps it is your God-given destiny (GGD)! Are you walking in it? Basking in it? If not, why? Stop, drop to your knees, and pray. Watch God eradicate all barriers! Whatever your grind (GGD), do it for the glory and honor of the most high God...grind baby, grind! Dr. Virginia A. Hines*

REFERENCES

Lerman, D. (2013). U.S. Military Vows to Put Women in Combat Roles by 2016. Retrieved from https: www.bloomberg.com/news/articles. Accessed on April 28, 2017.

U. S. Department of Veteran Affairs (USDVA). (2016). Federal Benefits for Veterans, Dependents, and Survivors. Retrieve from https://www.va.gov/opa/publications/benefits_book.asp. Accessed on May 2, 2017.

U.S. Department of Veteran Affairs (USDVA). (2017). Homeless Veterans. Retrieved from https://www.va.gov/homeless. Accessed on May 2, 2017.

U.S. Department of Veteran Affairs (USDVA). (2017). Homeless Veterans: Healthcare for Re-entry Veterans and Resources. Retrieved from https://www.va.gov/homeless/reentry.asp. Accessed on May 2, 2017.

U.S. Department of Veteran Affairs (USDVA). (2015). Military Sexual Trauma. Retrieved from https://www.womanshealth.va.gov. Accessed on May 2, 2017.

U.S. Department of Veteran Affairs (USDVA). (2016). Office of Suicide Prevention. Suicide Among Veterans and Other Americans. Press Release. Retrieved from https://www.va.gov/opa/pressrel/pressrelease. Accessed on May 2, 2017.

U.S. Department of Veteran Affairs (USDVA). (2015). Study of Barriers to Care for Women Veteran To VA Health Care. Retrieved from https://www.womenshealthva.gov/womenshealth/docs/women. Accessed on May 2, 2017.

U.S. Department of Veteran Affairs (USDVA). (2015). VA Caregiver Support. Retrieved from https://www.caregiver.va.gov. Accessed on May 2, 2017.

U.S. Department of Veteran Affairs (USDVA). (2016). VA Social Work: 90 Years of Excellence. Retrieved from https://www.socialwork.va.gov. Accessed on April 28, 2017.

U.S. Department of Veteran Affairs (USDVA). (2017). Women Veterans Health Care. Retrieved from https://www.womenshealth.va.gov. Accessed on May 4, 2017.

LINKS

Face Book: Virginia Hines
Website: cbivirtuouswoman.com
Foundation: saginawfoundation.org/site/carrie_hines/
Gospel CD: *In Memory of a Virtuous Woman: Carrie B. Hines (A Dedication CD)*
CD: cdbaby.com/cd/dvirginiahines (all proceeds continue to go to aforementioned foundation).
https://youtu.be/7JtclLhao-c video for Virtuous Woman
Dissertation Topic: Homelessness: Women veterans' perspective
https://saginawfoundation.thankyou4caring.org/hines

Proceeds from the sale of this book will be used to fund the next grind. Blessings and peace!

ABOUT THE AUTHOR

Dr. Virginia A. Hines is a grinder! She is currently a contemporary gospel singer, songwriter, philanthropist, gospel recording artist, and most recently an author. Dr. Hines served honorably in the U.S. Army for six years. She is currently employed with the Department of Veteran Affairs and has served in federal civil service for more than thirty-two years. Dr. Hines holds a PhD. in Human Services, a Master's Degree in Social Work, a Bachelor' Degree in Social Work, and an Associate's Degree in Pre-Arts.

Dissertation Topic: Homelessness: Women veterans' perspective.

Greatest Feats: A child of the Most High God. Daughter of the late great Carrie B. Hines. Developer of the Carrie B. Hines Scholarship Endowment.

Gospel CD: In Memory of a Virtuous Woman: Carrie B. Hines. A dedication CD with all proceeds submitted to the Carrie B. Hines Foundation (saginawfoundation.org/site/carrie_hines/ benefiting children enrolled in Big Brothers Big Sisters and Saginaw area high school seniors seeking access to scholarship dollars for college).

Glory to God!